HOLY FOOLS & MAD HATTERS

Beloved Pan and all ye other gods who haunt this place, give me beauty in the inward soul; and may the outward and inward person be at one.

—Plato, *Dialogues, Phaedrus*

HOLY
FOOLS
&
MAD
HATTERS

A
Handbook
for
Hobbyhorse
Holiness

EDWARD HAYS

Forest of Peace Books

Other Books by the Author:
(available from the publisher)

Prayers and Rituals
Prayers for a Planetary Pilgrim
Prayers for the Domestic Church
Prayers for the Servants of God

Contemporary Spirituality
A Pilgrim's Almanac
In Pursuit of the Great White Rabbit
Pray All Ways
Secular Sanctity

Parables and Stories
St. George and the Dragon
The Magic Lantern
The Ethiopian Tattoo Shop
Twelve and One-Half Keys
Sundancer
The Christmas Eve Storyteller

HOLY FOOLS AND MAD HATTERS

copyright © 1993, by Edward M. Hays

Library of Congress Catalog Card Number: 92-83893
ISBN: 0-939516-18-7

published by
Forest of Peace Books, Inc.
PO Box 269
Leavenworth, KS 66048-0269 USA

printed by
Hall Directory, Inc.
Topeka, KS 66608

first printing: February 1993

cover art by
Edward Hays

art consultation by
David de Rousseau

Other than the art on pages 30, 38, 55, 106, 120, 123 and 134 which were sketched by Edward Hays and those on pages 58 and 60, the graphics in this book are gratefully used with permission from the Dover Pictorial Archive Series, Dover Publications, Inc., New York. The graphics came from: Men, Jim Harter; Women, Jim Harter; Old-Fashioned Illustrations of Children, Carol Belanger Grafton; Treasury of Fantastic and Mythological Creatures, Richard Huber; Goods and Merchandise, William Rowe; Hands, Jim Harter; Food and Drink, Jim Harter; Old-Fashioned Transportation Cuts, Carol Belanger Grafton; Decorative and Illustrative Mortised Cuts, Carol Belanger Grafton; Picture Book of Devils, Demons and Witchcraft, Ernst and Joanna Lehner; Old-Fashioned Animal Cuts, Carol Belanger Grafton; The Dore Bible Illustrations, Gustave Dore; Humorous Victorian Spot Illustrations, Carol Belanger Grafton; 200 Decorative Title-Pages, Alexander Nesbitt; Animals, Jim Harter.

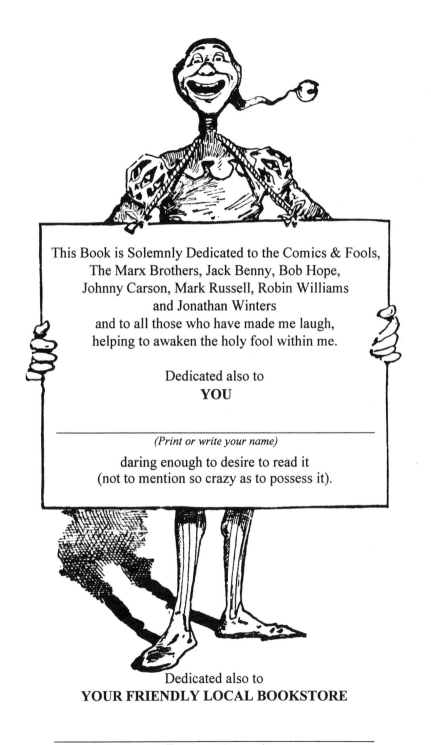

This Book is Solemnly Dedicated to the Comics & Fools,
The Marx Brothers, Jack Benny, Bob Hope,
Johnny Carson, Mark Russell, Robin Williams
and Jonathan Winters
and to all those who have made me laugh,
helping to awaken the holy fool within me.

Dedicated also to
YOU

_____

(Print or write your name)

daring enough to desire to read it
(not to mention so crazy as to possess it).

Dedicated also to
YOUR FRIENDLY LOCAL BOOKSTORE

_____

(Print or write name)

which was playful enough to display it
along with their books of serious spirituality.

THE DECLARATION OF DEPENDENCE

Let it be known to one and all: I hereby declare that this book would not have been possible without my dependence upon those friends who labored to edit it, worked to lay out the text in an appealing manner as well as juggle the hundreds of critical details so necessary for it to be printed, bound and distributed.

I declare to you, the reader or anyone else who may come upon it by chance, that this book would not have been possible without the efforts of **Thomas Turkle**, my tireless publisher, **Thomas Skorupa**, my ever patient editor, and his co-editors, **Paula Duke** and **Immanuel Eimer**, as well as the help of **Joanne Meyer** and **Johnny Johnston III** of Forest of Peace Books. Finally, I acknowledge, with no small debt of gratitude, **Steve Hall** and his staff of Hall Directory who printed this volume.

I further acknowledge the scholarship and assistance of the following: the writers & authors of Encyclopaedia Britannica, Volumes 4, 7, 9, William Benton, Publisher; Brewer's Dictionary of Phrase & Fable, edited by Ivor Evans, Harper & Row; The Best Book of Trivia, by V. Shei & Jack Griffin, Gallery Books; Parabola, Volume IV, No. 1 and Volume XII, No. 4; Fools, Clowns & Jesters, by Paul Cline, Green Tiger Press; Extraordinary Origins of Everyday Things, by Charles Panati, Harper & Row; The Rituals of Dinner, by Margaret Visser, Grove Weidenfeld Publisher; and the Works of Matthew, Mark, Luke and John. I am grateful to all the above and their publishers for the use of their works in the preparation of this text.

I solemnly declare not only my dependence but also my gratitude to those named above for their generous share in the publication of this small book on foolishness and holiness.

February 14, 1993

TABLE OF CONTENTS

The Story Begins

Murray had told me, "Wait for him by the big bend in the river—and be prepared!" My heart tap-toed with excitement as I arrived at the wide curve in the rushing river. With the broad strokes of a Michelangelo painting my mind had swiftly created a full-color image of Dhirananda, the spiritual master whom I would shortly meet. What a privilege it was to have this opportunity, since he only spent a few months each year down here on the prairie. The rest of the year he lived in solitude in his hermitage high in the mountains.

Seated on a rock by the river, I waited. As the hours passed, my mind's Michelangelo masterpiece began to flesh out as I conjured up the sound of Dhirananda's voice. I could see myself seated lovingly at the Master's feet, pondering his wisdom-filled question, "What is the sound of one foot dancing" or some other Zen-like riddle. Time rushed by with the speed of the river. As if brushing aside the nagging temptation of an ex-smoker, I resisted the desire to look at my pocket watch. Old habits, however, are harder than rocks to break, and I eventually gave in, pulling the watch from my pocket to check the time. I had been waiting for six hours!

Slipping my timepiece back into my pocket, I couldn't help but reflect on the fact that I had stopped wearing a wrist watch weeks ago. Not having one was symbolic to me. My bare wrist was a sign of my desire to be free. Free not only of the constraints of time, but of all the artificial systems that I felt enslaved me. However, I did need a few anchor times, and so I compromised by carrying a pocket watch. Now, both it and my body clock made me as restless as a race horse at the starting gate. I had spent most of the day waiting—and still no Dhirananda.

Having been pre-warned, however, I was prepared for anything. They had said that the old master, while very holy, could also be very "naughty," even rude. When people came seeking to become his disciples, he'd been known to throw rocks at them and colorfully curse them—in several different languages. If, like a hungry dog, they continued to follow him, he might offer to teach them, but would make the conditions so radical as to be nearly impossible. Knowing this, I felt prepared, ready for the test.

For years, it seemed, I had stumbled along. I had read a library of books on holiness and had tried various methods of prayer and meditation. Yet I was still on square one of the Game of Enlightenment. Murray had told me that Dhirananda knew the Way, having traveled it for years, and was a master guide. I don't remember what it was that had started the fire in me, but it had been burning—more like smoldering—in me for years. How I wanted it to blaze like a forest fire. What I needed was a practiced pyromaniac, a fire lover who knew how to make the dry timber of my soul explode with zeal. No cost seemed too great, no danger too risky, to stop me at this point.

What neither cost nor danger could do, however, boredom had. My mind was filled with somersaulting questions: "Am I at the wrong bend in the river? Maybe I misunderstood: was it today or tomorrow when the Master was to pass this way? Does he only travel at night?..." The river echoed the torrent of questions as its waters splashed around and over the rocks.

"Clipity clop, clipity clop, clipity clop. Whoaaa! Excuse me, stranger. Do you know what time it is?"

I looked up, shocked to see not an orange-robed holy man, but what appeared to be a smiling, senior—if not also senile—citizen. He was dressed in white tennis shoes, gray wash pants, a faded blue shirt and was riding a child's hobbyhorse! While he had a white beard, flowing white hair and deep, peaceful blue eyes, this was surely no holy man. His arrival on that hobbyhorse flunked every guru test of my mind's Michelangelo image.

"Yes," I said with some hesitation, pulling out my pocket watch, "it's 5:15."

Pulling the hobbyhorse out from between his legs, he inserted it in a white canvas bag which he had carried over one shoulder. As the hobbyhorse disappeared into the bag, he grinned at me. "Waiting for someone, or are you just a river watcher?" he asked playfully.

"I'm waiting for a famous holy man named Swami Dhirananda. I was told I might encounter him here at this bend in the river." My voice full of icy skepticism, I asked, "You wouldn't...ah...er...happen to be him, would you?"

"What a strange name, sounds rather Eastern! Do I look like someone from the Orient? No, I'm sorry, my name is Window Sill. Rather a nice sound to it, don't you think? I understand that some non-English speaking people consider it to be the most beautiful sounding word in the language. But back to your question. You say you're waiting for this, what was the name, Deer A Donna?"

"Dhirananda! Yes, I am. I've been waiting on this rock for almost seven hours now. Do you live near here, Mr. Window Sill?"

"Is this the first or second week of the month? If it's the second week, I've made a mistake. My name isn't Window Sill, but Cellar Door! You see I have several names, which may surprise you. Personal names are like clothing. Do you wear the same clothing everyday? If you do, it must be rather boring. It's the same with names. One should have a name for each season, as well as one for special occasions. Along with Window Sill, those of other tongues think that Cellar Door is one of the more musical names in English.

"I can tell just by the way you're looking at me that you, however, question that tasty tidbit of truth. Trouble is, you're like all the others. Yes, you're deaf to the beauty of words! It's a common affliction caused by the mind which robs you of the music of words."

Tapping his head, he continued, "Wonderful organ, but it forces you to associate a word with a common, colorless image. The result is that you become deaf to the melodic beauty of such names as Cellar Door."

"Sounds like a Country Rock band," I blurted out.

"Nonsense. Try this," he said. "Repeat it ten or fifteen times: Cellar Door, Cellar Door, Cellar Door, Cellar Door, Cellar Door. That was only five times, but now really listen to the melodic flow of it: *Cel-lar Door*! Ah, young man, it's like honey-spiced wine flowing across one's lips."

Slowly running the tip of his tongue across his lips, he looked heavenward as if he had just tasted a rare vintage wine. I had risen from my seat on the rock, hoping that this eccentric character would be on his way. If I hadn't been afraid of missing Dhirananda, I would have excused myself and left this strange passerby. I smiled, trying to look interested, and slowly repeated, "Cellar Door, Cellar Door, Cellar Door.... You're right, it is a beautiful sounding phrase. Now, Mr. Cellar Door, may I ask, did you see anyone as you came here? I'm waiting for...."

"Yes, you may ask. Ah yes, Dhirananda, a weird fellow from all I hear."

It was the way he said "Dhirananda," that suddenly sprang the trap. Of course, it *was* him! The realization struck me more tellingly than any Zen Master's stick could have. I glimpsed the sacredness beneath the eccentric surface. What a fool I had been! I wasn't prepared at all for him to look like, or act like, a senile senior citizen.

"Please excuse me, Dhirananda. You see, I've never seen a photograph of you! I had thought you would look...ah...er...different. I've been waiting here for you to ask if I could...if you would...."

"Forget it!" He quickly turned around, swinging his canvas bag over his shoulder, and jogged away along the river bank. Just as quickly, I gathered up my things and ran after him.

"Are you following me?" He turned and bellowed, "Beware of the dog!" As I drew close, he stopped and picked up a blanket roll laying next to a tree. He must have dropped it there before he came to the place where I was sitting by the river. Hoisting up the sleeping roll next to the white canvas bag on his shoulder, he glared at me, "What do you want?"

"I want...."

"Stop! Don't say another word. While knowing what you want is important, it's not as critical as asking, 'What are you willing to pay for it?' What you seek and what I have to offer is very expensive—and dangerous!"

"Yes, I'm willing to pay. But, I confess, sir, that I'm surprised that you charge. I wasn't aware that spiritual masters charged a fee for their wisdom and guidance. I'm not rich, but...."

"Not money, stupid! Money's easy to part with. When I say, 'expensive,' I mean that what you seek will cost what you treasure far more than money: T.P.P! Time, Practice and Patience—they're the great, ancient and holy trinity required of anyone seeking greatness. Unless you're willing to pay each of those in lavish amounts you're wasting my time, and yours."

He turned and began walking rapidly along the river, "Go away; as Marlene Dietrich said, 'I *vant* to be alone.' "

I had waited too long for this opportunity, and no amount of rejection or resistance would deter me now. It was like having a big fish on the line, and I didn't want him to get away. So I continued to jog behind him. "I understand, sir, about the cost of time, practice and patience. I am willing to give them in generous amounts, but what did you mean when you said that what I seek is dangerous?"

" 'The Way is narrow,' as Jesus said, 'and rough.' He was trying to warn those who thought his way would be a snap. In the Orient they say, 'The Way is as narrow as a razor's edge'! Ever walked anything *that* narrow? It's the same as mountain climbing: the higher you climb, the more dangerous it becomes. Have you calculated the full cost? If not, don't follow me like some lost puppy dog. Leave me alone. All this talking and all your questions—you're an environmental disaster. You're spoiling the beauty of this lovely evening. If you insist on accompanying me, then shut up!"

I counted silence a small price to pay for being with him, so I silently trudged behind him. Twilight was lowering her delicate blue-green veil on the forest, highlighted by the broad yellow shafts of the setting sun slanting through the woods. The fading golden light transformed the river into a deep purple torrent edged with luminous white foam and spray as it dashed over great gray-green rocks. Crickets added their voices to the river's song. My heart sang its own song of gratitude: I had found the Master! Not only had I found him, but had endured the first acid test. He had allowed me to follow him.

"Let's stop here," Dhirananda said. "This is a good place to spend the night. If you want to gather up some wood, we'll build a fire."

As the small fire ballooned a yellow-orange dome over us, I was delighted that he and I were visiting like traveling companions on the same bus seat. We drank hot tea and ate a little bread. It was a simple meal, and I carefully avoided any questions about spiritual things. I didn't mention prayer or holiness and tried to simply enjoy his presence. We fell silent as the flames slowly shrank into orange embers, then rolled up in our blankets and went to sleep.

The next morning I was awakened by a clinking sound. I opened my eyes to see him striking a spoon against a small teapot. "Morning tea, Sahib!" He had arisen before me, had built a small fire and had made breakfast tea. He smiled at me, but said nothing more as he sipped his hot tea.

In the crisp morning air of a new day, with tissue paper fog rising up from the river, wrapped in my blanket, I drank my tea and felt guilty. "I'm sorry, Master, that I overslept. It was I, not you, who should have made morning tea."

"Careful, you're beginning to talk like a disciple!" He winked at me. "If you still want to accompany me," he said as he walked down to the river to wash out the teapot, "then none of this *disciple* stuff! I don't want any disciples. I'm not that kind of teacher. There are those who need disciples, just as there are those who need masters. If you're interested in traveling with me, then we must be companions on the Way, and friends. So, just call me Charlie!"

"Charlie?" I was disappointed. I wanted to have my very own mentor, someone famous whom I could quote with pride. "As my Master once said to me...." I reluctantly agreed and promised, "Yes, if you will have me, I promise that I will not call myself your disciple. But somehow, sir, 'Charlie' seems too casual for a teacher. Couldn't I please call you 'Master'?"

"Master, Spot, Charlie or Window Sill! Today, however, I'd prefer

Cellar Door. But if you must call me Master—for now, mind you—I can bear up under that heavy-duty title. If you're going to call me Master, though, I fear I'll have to call you Nipper. Hmm…Nipper, not a bad sounding name for a disciple, come to think of it. Now, Nipper, my new friend, let's break camp and be on our way."

In silence, like the night before, we walked together for some time. I tried to be patient, waiting for an explanation about the name. However, in time, like an old shoestring, I snapped. "Tell me, Master, why did you rename me Nipper? Is it a Zen name or…?"

"Nipper," he said as he stopped and turned toward me, "remember the trademark of RCA Victor, the old record player with its brass horn and the white dog with black ears sitting next to it. The dog's head is cocked attentively to one side, and he has this fascinated look on his face."

"Yes, it's one of the world's famous trademarks, but I…."

"The original painting for that trademark was by Francis Barraud, and the dog's name was Nipper!" Slapping his thigh repeatedly, he roared with laughter. "Great name for a disciple, isn't it?"

I tried to smile, but it wasn't funny to me. After that, it was easier to walk in silence. Occasionally, he would break out into a laugh but said nothing more.

"Look at that!" I said, pointing to a gorgeous purple wildflower."

"Don't point, Nipper. It isn't polite! A simple nod of the head, a warm smile or a genuflection is sufficient to acknowledge someone or something of beauty. Didn't your mother teach you that it isn't polite to point! That goes for relating to all life forms, not simply people. How can you say you want to become enlightened if you've not mastered even the most fundamental of lessons?"

"I'm sorry, Master. I was taken aback by the beauty of the blossom, and I didn't want you to miss seeing such a striking flower.

"You know, what you said about not pointing reminds me of being in kindergarten. It's like starting at the very beginning."

"That's the point, Nipper. Walking the Way requires a 'Beginner's Mind,' and where else can you begin but at the beginning? Most seekers are too impatient for that. Those who wish to become holy need a handbook, like those old Children's Readers with lots of pictures. I have a hunch, my friend, that soon you will come upon such a handbook. Yes, if you wish to master the art of entering by the Narrow Gate, the art of walking the narrow razor's edge, the only place to begin is at the beginning."

With one eye closed and the other one blazing like fire, he asked, "Tell me, Nipper, why do you want to learn how to become holy?"

"Master, I seek enlightenment. I hunger for bliss, to be one with the Divine Mystery. I've read about the lives of saints and "enlightened ones" who can levitate, speak in foreign tongues, walk on water or fire, read minds and heal the sick. I would love to know how to...."

Before I could finish, he grabbed my elbow and yanked me to one side. "Watch out, Nipper, you almost slipped off the edge!" I was confused because I wasn't standing on any ledge or edge. I was walking on a wide path in the woods. Also, his grip was vice-like, and my heart pounded with fear at the thought that I had somehow made him angry.

"The hunger for miracles is more than dangerous, it's lethal! Many are those too eager for special powers who have fallen from the Way. Beware, seek nothing! Do not even seek a particular virtue. Seek with a passion only the Divine Mystery. Do not desire the powers of saints but desire only what they sought. And do so with trembling and fear."

We walked in silence for some time. Then, pausing, he said, "Nipper, whenever you meet other pilgrims of the Way, share with them whatever truth you have learned from the Narrow Path. Beware, however. You'll know when it's your duty to do so, or if you just want to parade your 'wisdom.' You'll also know if they're ready to hear what you've learned. If you perceive that someone is not a true pilgrim, or not prepared for the truth, be silent. Remember what Jesus said about your pearls?"

Upon cresting a hilltop, a valley appeared and the road we walked winded down into a village. I had no idea where the two of us were bound. Perhaps, I thought, this town might be our destination. "We'll enter that town up ahead," he said with a broad smile, his eyes dancing with glee as he placed his canvas bag on the ground. "The people there will ask the usual questions that folks ask of a holy man: the meaning of life, death and suffering—and sex, if they're religious folk! We must be prepared."

He winked at me, opened the white canvas bag and removed the hobbyhorse he had ridden when I first met him. Next, he pulled out of the bag what appeared to be a black silk pancake. With a flick of his wrist, it sprang into a black top hat, which he placed on his head. Then, straddling the wooden pole of the hobbyhorse, he seized the reins and reared backwards, whinnying like a horse. He playfully rode around me, waving the top hat with one hand. "Hi Ho, Gonnella. Come on, Nipper, my faithful companion, let's go!"

"Master, don't you mean 'Hi Ho, Silver'?"

"Nope, Nipper. I mean old Gonnella here, my skinny poled mount. The Duke of Ferrara had a household jester named Gonnella. The duke's fool rode a horse that was all skin and bone. The old bone-bag eventually got the jester's name and found his way into Cervantes' *Don Quixote*. Even Gonnella wasn't as skinny as my silly stud, though."

The Master roared with laughter as he rode in wild, erratic circles on his hobbyhorse. My heart suddenly locked gears with embarrassment. For the Master to enter the town like this would make us look like insane idiots. The townsfolk would think that we had escaped from some mental institution. Perhaps, I suddenly thought, this is another test for me. If it was a test of patience, of waiting for some explanation of this bizarre behavior, I had failed. "Master, this is insane! Why are we entering the town with you wearing that top hat and riding a child's hobbyhorse?"

"Because, my faithful companion, Nipper, we're God's Fools! The fact that this wooden horse is also a child's toy makes it all the better. It gets its name from the hobbled gait of children imitating a horse's canter," he said as he cantered horse-like in wide circles on the road. "Jesters, court clowns, rode hobbyhorses in Renaissance festivals, but it wasn't an original idea. Those jesters borrowed the idea from Muslim holy men. Yes, Nipper, hobbyhorses originated in Thirteenth Century Afghanistan where Sufi mystics used them. They traveled about in small bands as itinerant prophets, and whenever they entered a village, as we are about to do, they did so riding on these! They called themselves 'God's Fools.' They performed music, told mystical Sufi parables and preached the Way of truth to those assembled.

"Ah, Nipper, I see the question written in neon letters in your eyes: 'But why did those holy men enter villages riding on hobbyhorses?' They pretended to be idiots and fools so they could escape persecution! We will do the same."

Handing me his white canvas bag, he pretended to rear upwards, whinnying with obvious delight and shouting, "Clipity clop, clipity clop, it's off to play we go. Remember, Nipper, what the wise ones say: 'The arrival of a good clown will be better for the town than twenty asses laden with gold.' "

"Master, I...ah...ah..." I stammered.

"You're embarrassed to accompany me, Nipper? I thought you said you were eager to pay any price to be a disciple?"

"Yes, I did, but I didn't know...."

"Your face is growing red, my friend," he said as he stopped riding his hobbyhorse. Putting his arm around my shoulder, he said with great compassion, "Don't be shamed by your concern about looking foolish. It's usually one of the last things to fall away. When we're young, or even middle-aged, no one wants to appear foolish. Oh, a few dress up in silly clown suits and act the part. But everyone knows they're only temporarily acting out the role. Besides, it's really rather easy to hide behind a mask and costume. But to have people laugh at you because they think you're really stupid and silly, that's not so funny. True fools, Nipper, don't pretend—or wear clown suits; for them it's no masquerade. They've truly found the Path by being dumb-founded! With gray hair and age, it's easier to be divinely dumb and to act foolishly. People excuse such behavior, thinking you're a little senile or that you've 'earned' the right to be a little eccentric. Ah, but the serious guardians of order dread old holy fools."

"You're kind to excuse my embarrassment, Master, and I appreciate your saying that it becomes easier with age. But weren't there also young holy fools like Francis of Assisi who did outrageous things and were considered mad?"

"Yes, you're correct. Francis and many others who were not yet gray-heads found the secret to holy madness. Some say that the word 'silly' which comes from the Old English *saelig* means blessed and, by extension, holy. Francis and other saints were sacredly silly. You can be too! It only takes a little time and encouragement to allow the playful and humorous part of you to bite off the head of the worm inside named Pride. Holy Fools, Nipper, are folks who are fanatic about keeping the one great commandment to love God and neighbor as self. Having fallen in love with themselves—just as they are, with all their imperfections—they can take the risk that others may *not* love them. You're not alone in fearing to appear foolish. Nor are you unique in your low self-esteem. It's an almost universal affliction.

"Nipper, a good disciple is, first of all, obedient. Under holy obedience I order you to sit down and close your eyes. Good. Now with your eyes still closed open my white canvas bag that you're holding. Reach in the bag, about half-way down, and you'll feel a book. Pull it out of the bag, but don't open your eyes yet. The book in your hands holds a lot of secrets, and I want you to read it. Now I want you to count to sixty-six slowly and then open your eyes."

I did as he instructed. When I reached sixty-six, I opened my eyes. I was all alone! The master was nowhere to be seen. My heart sank to my socks. "He's gone!" I thought. "After all my efforts to find him, now I've lost him because I wasn't willing to look foolish." I glanced down at the book I had taken from the bag. It was as yellowed as an October oak leaf. While tattered and old, its title almost danced off the cover: *HOLY FOOLS AND MAD HATTERS, A HANDBOOK FOR HOBBY-HORSE HOLINESS*. Someone, perhaps the Master, had written in longhand under the subtitle, "A Reader for the Razor's Edge."

While disappointed, part of me was relieved that I didn't have to accompany him as he rode into town on his hobbyhorse. I decided to sit and wait, hoping for his return. Mindful of his request that I read the book, I found a comfortable position leaning back against a tree and opened the handbook to the first chapter.

Holy Fools

Are you among the one in six persons who bite their fingernails? And if so, do you belong to the one-third of the population who, statistically, are also toenail biters? While the anxious activity of fingernail biting might well invoke compassion, the image of a toenail biter is rather comical. It is a nervous habit which would seem to require the agility of a yoga master. Yet the thought of canonizing a toenail biter—or any other kind of eccentric—as a saint (the possibilities for a statue tickle the imagination) seems out of the question. In contemporary spirituality holiness and wholeness are frequently seen as Siamese twins. However, are holiness and wholeness really the same thing?

Wholeness suggests physical, mental and emotional completeness. It implies that you "have it all together," that you are sane as well as saintly. But is that a true notion of holiness? Benito Mussolini, the Fascist dictator of Italy, once said, "Anyone who has read the lives of the saints knows that they were all insane." The family of Jesus of Nazareth agreed with Mussolini when, as the Gospel writer Mark tells us, they came to take charge of Jesus, thinking that he was mad. But they were not alone, for the official religious establishment agreed, the only difference being that they laid the blame not on a mental disorder but on demonic possession (See Mk. 3: 21-22). From either viewpoint, the holiness of Jesus was not holistic.

Perhaps the identification of holiness with wholeness has arisen from our attempt to make religion a comfortable companion to our culture's ideals. As our secular society makes prayer and worship an endangered species, a desire for just plain, old-fashioned holiness is often seen as "weird," if not comical. Perhaps the interchange of holiness and wholeness is the result of our recent middle-class concern with well-balanced diets, good mental health and "healthy" living. Each of these is a worthwhile concern, but do they create a climate that fosters a fear about appearing in any way imbalanced?

A priest friend of mine recently lamented about the disappearance of the "characters," the eccentrics, the old pastors who once flourished in his youthful days as an assistant pastor. Think about it: where are the clowns? Not only with the clergy but in other walks of life, how many eccentrics do you know today? It isn't wholesome to be different, to have eccentricities, in a society that judges both your holiness and your mental health by how well you "fit in" with your community or society. When one lives in a very "sane" world, then being "out of step" with the accepted norms usually does appear as insanity. I am not talking about true mental illness, which is painful and destructive to life, but rather about "appearing" to be crazy because of how you live. One might call it a Messianic Madness which possesses those willing to clown around with the insanity of the world's values and power structures.

Not long ago, one such eccentric in England built himself an unusual home. The inside of his house looked like a typical outside: it had brick walls, exterior window frames and outdoor lighting fixtures. The furniture inside his home was patio furniture. The outside of his house on the other hand was wallpapered with framed pictures on all its walls. In short, it was an inside-out house. When people would ask him why he had built such a house, he would always reply, "I have chosen to live outside the Crazy House." Was this response just comical or was it also prophetic? By their ex-centricity, by being slightly to either side of center in behavior, holy fools and prophets mirror back for us a truth to which we are blind—or too fearful to acknowledge.

Jesus was such a clown. His words, stories and behavior fearlessly brought into focus the oppression of both the powerful Roman Empire and the Temple's religious establishment. His poor peasant listeners did not miss the humor in his parables which poked fun at the rigid structures of their society. I know that nowhere in the Scriptures will you find that Jesus laughed. But neither is there any record that he went to the bathroom! And just as I cannot conceive of a constipated Christ, I cannot conceive of a Christ who was *not* comical. Perhaps the authors of the Gospels didn't mention his humor since they believed that being the son of God excluded laughter and humor: God being holy but not humorous. Yet we humans are made in the image of God, so humor—so much a part of our humanity—must also, it would seem, be a godly trait.

There is a creation story in the lore of the Apache Indians which tells about how the Creator delighted in making the first humans able to do so many things. They could see, hear, talk, run, dance and create things with their hands. But God wasn't fully satisfied. Something seemed to be lacking in these wonderful new beings. And so the Creator went back to the creation studio and experimented with different possibilities. At long last the one final thing that was needed became clear: it was laughter! And when the first humans were given this essential new gift, they laughed and laughed. It was only on hearing this that the Creator said, "Now you are fit to be alive!" Like the misconception that Jesus never laughed, this story clears up any misguided notion about American Indians being humorless. Laughter was indeed central to the character of even the "Wild West" Indians. Despite the "stone-face" image passed on to us, laughter was a much more common sound than war cries in tribal villages.

In all the great religious traditions you will find an apostle of laughter, a prophetic clown, a trickster, a holy fool. Among the Native Americans he is called Coyote. In Buddhism there's good old Pu'tai, the fat and jolly wandering Zen monk who carried a big bag of trash on his back. Pu'tai would enter a village and empty his bag of bits and pieces of junk—a cast-off sandal or perhaps a broken bowl. With smiling solemnity he would announce, "What is this?" His clowning served to mirror how much junk we carry around in life, mistaking it for something of value. Islam also has had its share of holy Sufi clowns. And, like the desert mothers and fathers of early Christianity, the Hasidim have wonderful tales of comical rabbis who by their humor revealed the great wisdom of the Torah. Certainly Francis of Assisi was such a cosmic clown who took seriously St. Paul's words, "Let us be fools for Christ's sake."

Today, on the other hand, we are told, "For Christ's sake, stop being so foolish." If you step out of the culturally accepted pattern, you will be told, "'You can't buck City Hall,' why are you demonstrating against injustices? For Christ's sake, be reasonable!" Or you will be told to be patient, that change comes slowly, that you should surrender to the system. Yet Jesus wasn't patient with the oppressive, evil systems of his day. He rejected them in a non-violent yet direct way. You and I are invited to be fools, followers of the Great Fool, the Clown Christ. Wasn't he playing the classic clown when he got down on his knees and began washing his disciples' feet at the Last Supper? What better way was there to make his disciples see how comical was their desire for the sort of muscle exercised by the power brokers of the world. Prestige and privilege dissolved as they were anointed into humble servanthood. That was, and is, however, deemed foolishness in a world that values only power and pomp. Yet, in some way every disciple is ordained to servanthood and to foolhood, ordained to be a jester to the world.

At one time court jesters were an essential part of every court. Their function was not to make the king and the court laugh at jokes but rather to laugh at themselves! The fool served a real and necessary function of reminding the king of his follies, being his security guard against the loss of his humanity to the thieves of pride and power. He was an unofficial master of ceremonies who was free to break into loud laughter at a banquet in order to cut short a long-winded speech of some nobleman. The jester liberated the king from the stifling formal etiquette of his royal position.

Jesters and fools rush in where angels fear to tread. By their spontaneous approach to life they combine wisdom with madness or folly. As Shakespeare has said, "Jesters do oft prove prophets." Since neither kings nor popes, however, are often eager to welcome prophets, it is not surprising that fools were eventually abolished. The court jester and the saint were rejected because they frequently lacked the prudence to bow humbly before those in power. The position of a jester in royal courts and among titled households as a truth-teller and mirror had all but disappeared by the Seventeenth Century. King Henry VIII did away with the position of court jester—and no wonder, since his personal life wasn't exactly a joke. Queen Elizabeth I later had them classified in the same company with "Ruffians, Blasphemers, Thieves and Vagabonds." The Church had outlawed them centuries earlier, finding the clowns who mirrored popes, bishops, clergy and religion on the Feast of Fools to be "sacrilegious!" It isn't nice to make fun of those in power, especially those who hold "holy" power!

The clown also champions society's underdogs. Jesus was such a comic champion whose parables are often lost on us today because we lack a knowledge of the power structures of Jesus' day. His parables were humorous jabs that subtly revealed the truth about greedy landholders, the oppression of legalistic scribes and the pious parading of the Pharisees that passed for holiness. Jesus exposed the silliness of religious laws which were held out as divinely authored but only crippled the lives of the poor and powerless. He called his disciples to be fools who would mirror back the oppression of money lenders who were ready to take a poor person's cloak as security on a loan. Jesus said, "When they ask for your cloak, give them your shirt as well." (Mt. 5: 40). With both gone, stand before them naked so that you can mirror back to them the shame of their injustice! Such comical resistance to power is non-violent resistance. Laughter destroys evil without employing malice. As Samuel Johnson said, "Jest breaks no bones."

In our Twentieth Century wholesome holiness, where are the clowns? Where are the holy eccentrics, the fools for Christ's sake? How can we have a truly "whole" spirituality without merriment, without joyfully living in an inside-out house in the midst of a world that's a Crazy House? If any of the holy fools of history like Francis of Assisi or John the Baptist lived today, would they not be hospitalized or at least ushered into therapy? We dread appearing different from the rest of society in dress, speech or lifestyle. We lust for respectability more than freedom or holiness. But can we have either freedom or holiness and *not* be different from the rest of society? While there are indeed saints among us today, we seem to have a severe vocational shortage of holy fools and Christ-like clowns.

We do still have clowns in colorful circus costumes, but they are usually used for grand openings of fast-food stores. In most modern circuses clowns are used mainly to occupy the crowds, to fill the void before the next "big" act. The lack of real clowns and jesters has caused us to forget their symbolic power. We have forgotten the symbolism of the classic clown costume, divided in right and left halves, making a pattern of contrasts. That strange looking costume is really a vestment which illustrates how our humanity should be broad enough to include all contradictions. It speaks of how opposites can be blended into a mirthful, harmonious unity. The cap of the fool was originally conceived as a satire on the monk's cowl; the bell hanging on the end of it was an echo of the Sanctus bell of the Mass. The sacrament of the clown's costume seems to say, "Holy, Holy, Holy. God is present here in the laughter and merriment that consecrates our suffering and sorrows into joy."

In many clown skits, the right hand doesn't know what the left is doing, a division of self that pokes fun at a kind of behavior which each of us knows only too well. It is also a playful remembrance of the fool who follows Jesus' instruction that in giving alms to the poor your right hand shouldn't know what your foolish left hand is doing. To give away your hard-earned money isn't foolish to God, but it certainly is to those of the world.

In the name of an old Elizabethan play about a jester, *When You See Me You Know Me*, comes a challenge to our discipleship. That title implies that simply to see the jester was to know who s/he was. We should communicate who we are even in a simple glance. Can you pick out a fool for Christ's sake in a crowd, at a party or in a shopping mall? Do our lives, our homes, our styles of interaction at work reveal who we are—and who we are striving to be?

A real wholeness or harmony of life paradoxically must involve the disorder of the clown. The function of the trickster was to season order with disorder, seriousness with silliness, pomp with play, and so make life into a true whole. But such wholeness seems contrary to our contemporary understanding of holiness and wholeness. And so today the cosmic clown, the prophetic jester, is sadly absent from courts of both Church and State. Imagine the impact on our society if our president had a Cabinet post for the Secretary of Jest? Can you conceive the effect of a jester who would not hesitate to make fun of the lack of logic evident in so many government decisions? And what if the Pope had a Vatican court jester, a clown cardinal? S/he would be at the Pope's side at all times to keep those in the papal court from taking themselves too seriously. Would that every parish or city council had an official jester who would sit on the conference table and bite his toenails as all the officials wrung their hands worrying about this or that "terrible" problem.

At the Vatican or in the White House, at a school board meeting or a family crisis conference, a jester-clown's humor could awaken us to see what is really happening and could open our eyes to ingenious new ways of problem solving. The next time you find yourself faced with some "heavy" problem, allow the clown inside of you to come out, to help you laugh at yourself and "lighten up."

Historically, folly and clowning thrive in times of transition, such as New Year beginnings, on the Mardi Gras days before Lent begins, the crossing points of the seasons, birthdays and initiation rites. Crossing from the old to the new has traditionally required foolishness like reversing social and religious hierarchies, violating rules and cultural taboos, changing sexual roles; in short, providing a mirror vision to our normal life.  Imagine what insights parents might receive if at a birthday party the children pretended to be parents and the parents took on the roles of children! As we enter a new millennium, we are living at one of history's great transition points. Today more than ever we need clowns, not circus clowns but jester-trickster-prophetic clowns. The question is whether this deeply human vocation can be resurrected from the respectability and gentility that has embalmed middle-class Christianity? Is it possible to defossilize St. Paul's call for each of us to become a fool for Christ?

As organized religion lusts for solemn orthodoxy, as we become more and more mechanized by our increasingly computerized culture and dehumanized by the multiplication of bureaucracies, we need clowns more than ever before. As we find ourselves divided into opposing militant camps over countless ecological, moral, political, sexual and racial issues, can we embrace all the polarities of these issues in a seamless fabric of society—just as the jester's costume is a balanced pattern of contrasting colors and designs? Perhaps this generation will produce a cast of comical prophets to show the way, for historically whenever humanity has been faced with a grave crisis, it has proven an ability to rise and face the challenge. Why should today be any different? Why shouldn't it happen, especially if *you* are willing to be considered a bit eccentric, if you are willing to live out your discipleship with good humor and laughter?

Exercise and Reflection:

HOW TO BE YOUR OWN COURT JESTER

The next time you feel caught up in some problem which has you upset or worried, call in the clowns. Exaggerate the issue as much as you can: "Oh, God, this is the WORST thing that has **EVER** happened to me. It's worse than the San Francisco earthquake of '89!"

Then you might pound your head in clown's jest, weep fake tears, throw yourself on the floor...then have a good laugh. Be both audience and clown. When you're finished, you may not only feel better, but the issue or problem may find its proper proportion in your life.

JEWISH HUMOR

If you wonder whether Jesus was humorous as well as holy, remember that he was a Jew! From the very beginning of time Jews have been very funny people, able to laugh at themselves, at their fate—and at God! Jews still await the coming of the Messiah, and their more than 3000 years of waiting has given birth to such humor as we see in the following story:

In a small Russian village there lived a rabbi who had a strong vision that the Messiah—blest be God's name—was passing through that very part of Russia. Fearful that the Messiah might easily bypass such a small village, the people constructed a tall lookout tower on the main road. They then hired a man to sit in the watchtower to look for the Messiah's arrival. One day a friend stopped and called up to him, "How do you like your job?" The watchman yelled back, "The pay's not much...but it's steady work!"

Mad Hatters

Professional **fools and jesters** have appeared in all times and in all places. Like monks, religious, soldiers and police, fools also had special clothing which identified them as official jesters. Unlike professional religious, however, fools' clothing changed considerably from time to time.

Usually among the jester's attire was a motley coat of many colored patches and tight breeches with one leg a different color from the other. The fool wore a cap which resembled a monk's cowl and often had asses' ears on either side and a cockscomb on the top. From his cap and other parts of his attire hung small bells. The classic foolscap often had a conical shape, the same style as that worn by dunces. Besides making the fool easily identifiable, the cap eventually became a symbol of the jester's important social function.

Hats generally were once far more important than they are today since head coverings were statements about a person's social position and spirituality. While most of us are unaware of it, religious art, nine out of ten times, shows Jesus "indecently" dressed: his head is uncovered!

Through the marvel of television, the Near East almost daily visits our living rooms. Political unrest in the area, the specter of terrorism and the ongoing oppression of Palestinians in Israel have made us more aware of Near East culture. If you look carefully, you will notice that the heads of male orthodox Jews and Moslems, indoors or out, are always covered! A Jew's black hat or skullcap, a yarmulke, or the Arab's desert head scarf, is a sign of respect before God. Since God is everywhere, head coverings are worn at all times. That Jewish-Islamic spiritual tradition should challenge each of us who proclaims that the Kingdom of God is here among us to have some constant reminder of our faith.

This ancient spiritual practice has its roots in Sacred Scripture. In chapter twenty-one of the book of Leviticus is the command, "The priests shall not make bare the crown of the head...to their God they shall be sacred" (Lv. 21: 5-6). At the time of Jesus, the Pharisees took upon themselves the ritual requirements of the priesthood. Jesus, being a devout Jew, therefore, always would have covered his head in order to be decently attired.

That being the case, we might gain a unique insight into the personality of Jesus by imagining him wearing a black top hat! It would be no ordinary top hat, however, but a crazy one like the Mad Hatter's in *Alice in Wonderland*. Jesus the Mad Hatter would open our eyes to the fact that he often seemed as crazy as the Mad Hatter in Lewis Carroll's Tea Party. What made Jesus appear so eccentric to many was his profound belief in God's actual presence here and now. For him this radical awareness of God in every person and event was more than a dogma; it was a belief that shaped his lifestyle.

Mark's Gospel tells us that the relatives of Jesus came to "take charge of him, saying, 'He is out of his mind!'" Uncles, aunts and cousins all agreed that Jesus had "lost his marbles" and "wasn't playing with a full deck" and so decided that the boy belonged at the funny farm (See Mk. 3: 21-22). We need images of Jesus wearing a Mad Hatter's top hat—especially we "proper" middle-class Americans. We who long for acceptance from others, for respect, need to be reminded that the real Jesus appeared to the "important" people of his life as loony as the Mad Hatter!

While this reflection about the kinsfolk of Jesus viewing him as emotionally imbalanced may be mildly interesting, some of you are probably asking, "What has all this to do with my life, with my struggles in prayer and meditation, my quest for holiness?" Jesus said that "your foes will be those of your own household" (Mt. 10: 36). Ah, strange, but true! Isn't it our families that usually block our path to greatness, who hold us back from becoming what we could become? Jesus' family thought he was nuts since he walked away from a good business as a carpenter—and for what? Being a village craftsman brings good money and security. Why leave it for pie in the sky, for impractical God stuff? It wasn't even like the son of Joe and Mary had gone up to Jerusalem to become a temple scribe, part of the respectable religious establishment. No, the poor boy went off on some wild-holy-goose chase.

The personal application is that each one of us is family to someone. How do you respond when a child, a cousin or even a parent proposes to go off and do something "crazy"? That diagnosis usually means a choice lacks middle-class security, safety and the promise of a "future." Furthermore, what if you yourself make God stuff as important in your life as your business or profession? When religion becomes central, you are usually seen as a fanatic, as one who has lost touch with reality.

An earnest practice of prayer and spiritual disciplines—and actually living the values of the Gospel—are "properly" reserved only for Sundays or for those living in remote monasteries or behind convent walls.

If you and I took the invitations of Jesus seriously—did the things he did, lived the kind of life he called his disciples to live—I promise you that most of our families and friends would say that we had "lost our marbles." Consider doing anything other than working hard on life's great assembly line and, as a modern day Mad Hatter, you'll probably be scooted off to a shrink for realignment. Whenever prophets appear, walking boldly in response to the divine voice they hear in their hearts, the typical response is to quickly neuterize them by saying, "Oh, she's a saint!" or "He's really crazy!" Such labels of holiness or insanity excuse us from having to ask ourselves why our lives are not radically holy.

"Love your enemies" (Mt. 5: 44); "Anyone who wishes to be the greatest must remain the lowest, the servant of all" (Mk. 9: 35); "Enter through the narrow gate. The gate that leads to damnation is wide" (Mt. 7: 13): the teachings of Jesus are as illogical to prudent people as Lewis Carroll's Tea Party in *Alice in Wonderland*. Hosted by the mad March Hare, along with the Mad Hatter and the Dormouse, this outdoor tea party is really an insane affair where everyone is crazy except for Alice, a proper Victorian English girl. Like you and me, Alice presumes there should always be answers to questions, but those asked by the Mad Hatter don't have any! Logical little Alice says to the Mad Hatter, "I think you might do something better with time...than wasting it in asking riddles that have no answers." The Mad Hatter responds, "If you knew time as well as I do...you wouldn't talk about wasting *it*! It's a him!"

Jesus also asked crazy riddles that left his listeners searching for answers which seem impossible to find. "What is the profit, the bottom line," he asked, "if you win the whole world but lose your soul in the process?" (Mk. 8: 36). The seemingly insane logic of life is that life's most important questions lack answers! So, perhaps the best course of action is to be prudent. Don't waste your time asking yourself such riddles.

Lewis Carroll's wonderful choice of the Mad Hatter as a symbol for insanity was inspired by the dangerous Nineteenth Century profession of hat maker. Making men's felt hats required the use of mercurous nitrate. Its fumes in time caused a condition called St. Vitus' Dance, an uncontrollable bodily shaking which often was misinterpreted as a fit of madness. There is also a theory in literary circles that the colorful character of the Mad Hatter was loosely based on a certain Seventeenth Century English eccentric named Robert Crab. Reportedly Crab gave away all his possessions to the poor. He also lived very simply and was a strict vegetarian, eating nothing but leaves and grass. Certainly anyone who suggests giving away all one's property to the poor would have to be mad. Furthermore, anyone foolish enough to take such a proposal seriously would surely be mad as a hatter!

On the same day that Jesus' family came to "take charge of him," he was expelling evil powers out of the afflicted. At the same time, the scribes, the guardians of the religious establishment, arrived. Those scholars of the Law of God passed judgment on him, adding to his family's charge of insanity a more serious one. The scribes said, "This Jesus is more than mad, he's *possessed* by the Devil" (Mk. 3: 22)! We who fear the opinions of society and religious authorities think twice before following the voices we hear in our hearts. Most of us are eager to "shape up," to conform to society's norms. The cosmic twist is that Jesus and eccentrics like Robert Crab, like General George Booth who founded the Salvation Army or like Francis of Assisi, who went naked in his desire for absolute poverty, aren't possessed! It's not the Joan of Arcs in our world who are possessed; rather it's we of the middle of the road majority who are possessed by the Beelzebub, the Demon, of Respectability.

Another paradox, a comical cosmic somersault, is that if we wish to escape the demons that restrict our freedom, we will need the assistance of another demon! We will need the daimonic to escape the diabolic. Before you have a stroke at such an idea, consider the important distinction between the daimonic and the diabolic. The daimonic, as the ancient Greeks viewed it, is an inferior divinity—a dark, primal force, a genius spirit that lives in  the cellar of human consciousness. The diabolic, which originally meant "to divide or separate" is the daimonic out of control, thus become evil. Fearful of all that is dark and dangerous, in our zeal to cast out the devil, we have also closed the cellar door on the creative dark energies of the daimonic. The cost has been a dullness of life. "Angels are boring until they fall," says the psychologist Rollo May. Lucifer is just another one of millions of boring angels until he falls and becomes one of the most fascinating of creatures. Lucifer refuses to "knuckle under." He's an expression of independent self-assertion. Lucifer is a symbol of the urge for growth and self-determination so apparent in the personality of Jesus of Nazareth. The scribes and priests were right: Jesus was possessed! Why else would a village carpenter be so bold as to call himself a Son of God? Why else would he be so self-assured as to teach the truth even at the cost of respectability. Would that you and I were so possessed!

Rollo May adds that it's the child who is a "little angel" for too long that parents should worry about! Yes, worry if she's still a little angel at twenty-five or forty-five! The child who's a "little devil," on the other hand, gives parents a promise for good future development. Reflecting on that, perhaps we can see Eve and Adam's disobedience in Eden as not all bad! Didn't Jesus also disobey God's laws, those he considered to be idols and crippling to human growth? His Eve-like disobedience was a major source of conflict with the priests and scribes. Jesus was a little devil, disobedient to those laws that separated, that determined who should eat, work and pray together, that placed more importance on the means than the end. Even to this day, he calls you and me to be his disciples and to be little devils.

We are challenged by Jesus' words and life to three types of disobedience which require the courage of the little devil in us. The first is non-violent, civil disobedience when the state or society require a prophetic witness. The second is social-family disobedience whenever we must act contrary to the wishes or even demands of those closest to us. The third is sacred disobedience, which is not so much breaking the law as simply stating that we are "out-laws," outside the law because we are in-Christ! Deep prayer, thoughtful reflection and direction are, of course, necessary before acting in any one of these three ways.

In each of us is a fallen angel, maybe more than one! A fallen angel holding hands with a non-fallen one can give us the gift of demolition! Hand in hand, dark and light powers within give the passion necessary to exorcise the diabolic possession of "What will the neighbors say?" They can blow a hole in that velvet prison of possession of "What will Mommy say?" Without passion we can never escape. Without passion we can never pray as we ought to pray. All passion, however, is an expression of one's fallen angel. At the same time, all passion is a kind of possession! That's the reason the religious establishment and each of us are so afraid of it!

Sweet, proper Alice in Carroll's wonderful story wants life's tea parties to be played according to *proper* etiquette. Pious, sanctimonious Alice never does anything wrong; she is all sweet- ness and light. Poor, cramped Alice never asks any questions for which there are no answers. Sweet, obedient Alice, so concerned about what's proper, forever a prisoner in her cage, is *us*!

Salvation, once upon a time, meant liberation. Jesus came as a non-institutional savior to throw open our cage doors, to cut our apron strings, to liberate us not by black magic, but by white magic. The scribes charged that it was by black magic, by devil-power, that Jesus "de-deviled" those possessed by physical, psychic and spiritual ills. Jesus said, "You're the crazy ones! God's Spirit frees people! The spirit of evil, true diabolic power, imprisons! Whatever imprisons you, even if it is dressed up like an angel and quotes Holy Scripture, is diabolic!"

The Messianic Mad Hatter, Jesus the Magician, stands before you even as you read this chapter and is eager to work upon you a little of his white magic of the Spirit. The Messianic Magician doesn't pull a rabbit out of his black top hat, but rather a key! He offers you the key to the cage door where you and your talents, gifts and unique life-mission are held prisoner by the Arch Demon of Respectability. Also standing guard at your prison door are the demon of excessive security and childhood needs for acceptance. Each time you come to authentic prayer or worship you are offered the key to your prison. All you have to do is choose to be "crazy" enough to use it!

Your fears to reach out and take the key are more than understandable. Living as creatively and independently as Jesus can be very vulnerable and requires great trust. The following prayer may be of some assistance in unlocking your fears:

> Come, Holy Spirit,
> Come, Spirit of Madness
>   that possessed Jesus
>   and made him so passionate,
> Come and take possession of me.

As you ponder whether to use the key offered you—or even to pray such an insane prayer—recall the words of author Dr. Scott Peck. He said that Jesus' words, "Many are called, but few are chosen," should really be, "Many are called, but few choose!"

Exercises and Prayer:

THE ART OF DEMONETIZING

While the usual definition of demonetize is "to divest coins or bills of their monetary value," it also can be a spiritual discipline. We can divest our demons of their value or power by laughing at them. We can scoff at their sneaky suggestions to "take the sensible, financially secure way" or "stand up for your rights." The sly demons of security are especially fond of making your rights, not your duties or response-abilities the central focus. Another way to demonetize is to challenge a demon to an arm wrestling contest with a good angel. Regardless of the demon's dirty tricks, if you align yourself with Jesus, the Arch Mad Hatter, there is no doubt who will win.

A PRAYER FOR THE FOOLSCAP OF JESUS

The soldiers now led Jesus away into the hall known as the praetorium; at the same time they assembled the whole cohort (the audience). *They dressed him in royal purple* (as an idiot emperor), *then wove a crown of thorns* (a foolscap) *and put it on him. They began to salute him, "All hail! King of the Jews!" Continually striking Jesus on the head with a reed* (his scepter) *and spitting at him, they genuflected before him and pretended to pay him homage. When they had finished mocking him...* (Mk. 15: 16-20).

O, Christ the Cosmic Clown, you dared to be God's Fool
    and became a laughingstock and a scapegoat.
Help me, your disciple.
I fear the laughter of others
    and am unwilling to be the scapegoat for others' sins and faults.

Jesus the Jester, after your arrest
    the Sanhedrin temple guards blindfolded you.
Slapping you, they taunted you,
    "Play the prophet; which one struck you?"
Some ancient images of the Fool show the joker blindfolded
    to symbolize his ability to act not by sight
    but by insight, by intuitive wisdom.

O Blessed Blindfolded Jesus,
    teach me, so afraid of ridicule and mockery,
    the wisdom to embrace pain and tragedy
    as part of the Play of Life.
Teach me your trick of how to rise above the horselaughs,
    how to leap from the pit of self-pity.

Jesus, the Holy Fool, blindfold my eyes to insults
    so that I can see only with eyes of love,
    so that I may never return injury for injury.

Amen.

On some Tarot cards, the Fool is shown as the Hanged Man, suspended not by the neck but rather by one foot. That type of hanging was known as "baffling." It was an old punishment for debtors and traitors in parts of Europe. Baffling was a formal humiliation, the type inflicted on Jesus while he was mocked as the sacred king-victim.

AN EXORCISM FOR THE DEMON OF "WHAT WILL THE NEIGHBORS SAY?"

This common household devil lurks behind our lace curtains or hides in the grass of a well-mowed front lawn. From its hiding place it tries to torment us by threatening (usually in frightening echoes of parental voices) to expose us and to destroy our neighbors' good opinion of us.

The Exorcism: Seize the little devil by its tail and out loud ask yourself this question, "If I do what I want, what will my friends who love me say?" Then add, "As for those who are only onlookers, curiosity seekers or gossips, who the hell cares what they think or say!" Repeat this Prayer of Exorcism as often as needed until you are free of the demonic possession.

Clowning with Death

Jesus **instructed his disciples,** as have other spiritual masters, not to be foolish and let Old Bony Death catch them asleep. "Stay awake, be on guard like night watchmen!" (See Mt. 24: 4, 42). While this is a solemn, sober instruction, jesters have danced around its edges and broken social taboos by treating death as a joke. The clown, although not necessarily a courageous creature, does appear to be fearless. Court fools, who frequently dared to ridicule their kings, were protected by their supposed ignorance and madness. They had to face an even greater power in jest when confronting death. Fools and clowns survive encounters with even the most awesome powers by standing outside of fear. As if by magical miracles they sidestep every accident to emerge as triumphant, even if slightly disheveled in the process.

The wise fool is one who can play around with death and so walk the True Way. The Prophet Mohammed answered like a wise fool when asked, "What is the Way?" He said, "Live today as if it were your last day. Live today as if you would live a thousand years. In between those two ways is The Way." A parable about Ireland may help us to better grasp this wisdom.

In the late 1840's, Ireland was an island of misery. The potato famine, starvation, disease, harsh oppression by the English and emigration reduced the population by two million.

One gray day in county Limerick, a messenger came running up to the small whitewashed cottage of Michael and Margaret O'Reilly shouting, "Michael, his Lordship, the Knight of Glin, wants to see you at once!"

"Oh, Michael," cried Margaret, as he put on his cap and coat to leave with the messenger, " 'tis bad news his Lordship will be tellin' you—that we're next to be evicted. We'll be forced to join the long lines of the homeless. Oh, God, what will happen to us?"

Two hours later, however, Michael returned home jubilant. He told his wife that his Lordship had offered to pay his passage to America! The Knight of Glin, unlike the other landowners, did what he could to care for his tenant farmers in the midst of the great potato famine. They all agreed that Michael would go first, and after getting settled in America he'd send for Maggie and the kids.

Maggie asked, "When will you be leavin,' Michael?"

"That's the only hitch, Maggie dear. You see, with the ships so crowded and passage so difficult these days, it's necessary, his Lordship said, for me to be standin' by. His Lordship said he wouldn't know in advance when my passage would be available. I need to be ready to go at a moment's notice. So, Maggie, my love, it could be tomorrow or within the very hour."

Michael and Maggie set to work at

once and packed an old battered suitcase so that he would be ready to leave whenever his Lordship's messenger might come. Michael, not wanting to miss his turn, never left the house without his suitcase. The first time he entered the village pub carrying it and was asked where he was going, he responded, "I'm standin' by. I'm on my way to the Land of Promise, America, and I might get the word to leave this very hour. I wouldn't have time, y'see, to go home to get m'bag, so I'm carryin' it with me."

The days quickly passed, but Michael never went anywhere without his old battered suitcase. Mindful that he might receive word any moment that passage was available, he treated every visit with neighbors or friends as if it were the last. From the day he began to carry his suitcase, his favorite adjective was "precious." After viewing a rainbow over the village or finishing a simple evening meal with Maggie and the kids, he would exclaim, "Ah, precious! What a treasure!"

The days of waiting turned into weeks, but Michael lost none of his excitement about emigrating to the "Land of Promise," as they all called America. Whenever he would be invited to a wedding or asked to do something "next week," he would always respond, "Well, God willin', I'll be here. You know, I'm standin' by." As a result, all the villagers of Glin looked upon their neighbor as the village zany, calling their friend who always carried a suitcase, "Michael Standin' By." He  didn't mind the humorous name. In fact, he told Maggie it only helped him to stay alert, ready to leave at a moment's notice.

One month to the day after his Lordship's messenger had come to their small cottage, a neighbor, Thomas Meehan, came by asking if Michael could help him put up hay. It looked like it might rain, and the hay was ripe and ready. Michael grabbed his suitcase and told Maggie, "I might not have another chance to do a favor for m'friend Tom. I best go at once." He kissed her goodbye with the same intensity that characterized his life ever since the suitcase had become his constant companion. As Mike climbed onto Meehan's wagon with his suitcase, the other men greeted him with good-humored joking, "Welcome aboard, Michael Standin' By, 'tis to the hay field not the Land of Promise that we be goin' today." But he only smiled and laughed. Looking back at Maggie standing in the doorway of their small cottage, he waved as he repeated to himself, "Precious, precious."

In the middle of the afternoon, as dark rain clouds swept down low over the hills along the river Shannon, Margaret saw Tom Meehan's wagon, loaded with hay, pulling into the yard. Tom, with cap in hand, was at the door when she opened it. "Maggie, I'm sorry, but...."

"Tom, I know what you're goin' to say. Michael's no longer standin' by, is he? Well, he was more ready to go than any of the others on his Lordship's waitin' list."

"Right you are, Maggie, he was more than ready to go." Tom Meehan turned slightly and stepped a bit to the side. As he did, she could see the hay field workers carrying the body from the wagon to the cottage.

Dr. John Pilch, a scriptural scholar, has written about how certain cultures regard the different stages of time. Some place a great deal of value on the past. As a result they are less inclined to change, less open to what is new. They revere old things and customs. Other cultures, such as the Palestinian culture of Jesus and present-day third world countries treasure the present. They are not inclined to plan for the future and tend to be spontaneous. They have an enhanced capacity to enjoy life in the present moment. On the other hand, the type of time that most Westerners, particularly Americans, value most is the future. They tend to make judgments based on the future and are fond of making plans. They also usually lack interest in history or the past. Change and newness are easily embraced, and they tend to be impatient when reforms are delayed. They believe that the hope of tomorrow is in our youth and not in the wisdom of older people. The paradox is that while the American culture values the future, it is in a conspiracy to deny the most important future event: death!

The United States' neighbor to the south, Mexico, is a present-time culture. Again, it is paradoxical that while Mexican people tend to value the present more than the future, they have a great appreciation of death. Each year at the end of October—the same time as Americans are celebrating Halloween—Mexicans observe a week's festival called, *El Dia de Muertos*, "The Day of the Dead." It is an honored occasion for individuals to remember the dead of their families, and culturally it is a time to play around with death. It is an opportunity to realize that death daily walks right alongside each one of us.

Among the "holy" folk objects from that festival is one which shows death coming to a brick mason while he is at work building a wall. Mexican culture has countless such toys, playful images of death visiting people during various moments of daily life. These folk images resemble the death art of the late Middle Ages. Each year at Halloween, it is customary in our culture to display images of skeletons, but they are static images and not playfully shocking. Another interesting "holy" death toy is a type of deadly Jack-in-the-box. It's a small cardboard coffin which has a string coming out of the bottom. When the string is pulled, the lid of the coffin flips open and death, dressed as a skeleton, pops out of the coffin. To such delightfully un-American folk objects, a typical response might be, "Don't play around with death; don't joke about something so terrible." It's difficult to imagine us Americans, a future-oriented people, playing around with such holy death toys.

Jesus, describing the Age of God, spoke about someone who found a treasure in a field. The man hid it, went home and sold all he owned and bought the field. Life for those whose time zone is the Age of God is a treasure hunt. Remember the childhood books with the old pirate maps on which an "X" marked the spot of the buried treasure? Consider the implications if an "X" were on your house, room or apartment. First of all you would need a daily reminder to keep your eyes open for the treasure. Death Toys can effectively remind us of the treasure that is hidden right in front of us. Every field, every back yard, can hold a hidden treasure for those whose vocation is to be a Treasure Hunter. Life is a treasure hunt, in which the prize worth a fortune is life itself as it unfolds in each moment.

Sadly, most of us are blind to the treasure. Our vision would be healed instantly if wherever we went we carried a suitcase. We would not miss the wonder of life if, like Michael in the story, we were always on stand by. It was Michael's unique position of "standin' by" that transformed everything commonplace into the "precious." Daily life isn't precious or a treasure for us because we deny that we're "standin' by." We deny that we are also on his Lordship's Waiting List for the Promised Land. To live with such consciousness is to possess the pearl of wisdom.

To be mindful that life is a treasure hunt is to have the wisdom of Solomon, who didn't ask God for riches but for a heart wise and understanding. If you understand the shortness of life, if you appreciate how precious is each passing moment and experience of life, then you're as wise as was old Solomon. Regardless of how high your I.Q. might be, not to possess that wisdom is to be a fool. If you and I are to be truly wise, we will need constant wake-up calls to open our eyes to the hidden treasure, buried right in front of us.

One such reminder could be an old suitcase placed in a central position in your bedroom or your prayer corner. Since we so easily become blinded to whatever is ever present in our lives, you may have to move it to a new position every few days. Each time you look at the suitcase, you can say to yourself, "Since I'm standin' by, I had better enjoy even the smallest things today while they're still here." I assure you that if this is your abiding attitude, you *will* find treasures you never guessed existed hidden right in the midst of your daily life.

If you don't mind your co-workers calling you eccentric, you can carry your suitcase to work! After all, treasures can be found there just as well as at home. Along with being a reminder to live each day as if it were your last, the suitcase symbol will also prompt you to pack something in it. Pack it with the treasures you've found hidden in your back yard, at work or in a casual visit with a friend. Pack your suitcase daily with the only treasures you can take with you, the only treasures that customs will allow you to carry across the border.

Your "standin' by" suitcase could become a new religious image. You may say, "Not another one, we already have too many!" It's a great paradox that the most important religious symbol of Christians is the cross or crucifix. No other religious people have a symbol of death as their major holy image, yet are Christians any more awake to their death? No other religion in the world celebrates a Sacred Meal of Death, yet does your attendance at the Lord's Supper call you to treasure life more deeply? Does celebrating the Last Supper lead you to appreciate each passing moment of life? Ironically this failure to live with a holy consciousness of death may be the result of our Christian Arch-Belief in the Resurrection.

That belief in life beyond death, when married to our cultural denial of death, often causes a short circuit in consciousness. As players in life's Great Treasure Hunt, we can thus easily become losers-weepers instead of finders-keepers. A daily mindfulness of death is a counter-cultural consciousness. It is also a key element in a sound spirituality. It holds enormous power for personal conversion and change. It further reminds us not to take each other for granted, not to miss moments of beauty and grace or opportunities to do good.

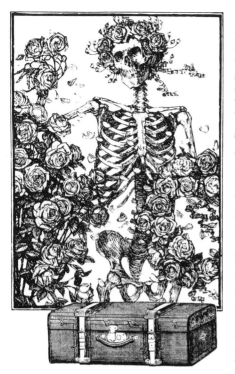

In olden times, it was customary for monks and other religious to keep a tangible reminder of death always before them by placing a human skull on their desks. Like its vivid mother death-reminder, the crucifix, with time the skull ceased to be a shocking reminder. Be careful, then, for the same deadly fate can await you if you choose to employ the consciousness-raising symbol of a sacred suitcase. Be diligent; always attempt to see that symbol with fresh eyes. If you frequently move it around in your home and carry it in your car, it can help open your eyes to countless precious moments and innumerable buried treasures.

If you use it well, your suitcase symbol will assist you in seeing the "X" that marks the spot of the hidden treasure which is written large over *everything*!

Exercise:

CENTERING OR OFF-CENTERING PRAYER?

Does Centering Prayer or meditation lead to being centered, perfectly balanced and well adjusted? If Jesus prayed that way, why did he appear to both family and foe as ex-centric? Should not any good prayer, silent or otherwise, lead to a different lifestyle—even when it appears as strange as Michael Standin' By's? Since most of us as children feared the laughter of playmates or classmates, it's not easy to embrace the call to radical discipleship, the call to be a holy eccentric.

While Centering Prayer opens the ears of the heart so one can hear God, it's so easy to forget what is heard as soon as we rise from prayer. This "instant" forgetfulness is the result of our fear of appearing to be strange—even slightly crazy.

At the heart of the concentric circles of deepening prayer is a call to prophetic witness which historically has been viewed as either madness or extreme eccentricity. Remember what you hear in your silent prayer and then boldly step off the edge! Such "off-centering prayer" is a marvelous way to quicken your appreciation of the Treasure in your midst.

A Joker Card in the Mail

Some **say it was** the gypsies, others the Tartars, Saracens or returning Crusaders, who introduced playing cards into Europe sometime during the Thirteenth Century. Most believe that, like so many creative inventions, they came from the Far East, China or India. Playing cards appeared in China almost at the same time as paper money, the two being nearly identical in their early forms. While cards today are employed primarily for play and for gambling, originally they were utilized as aids in divination. Playing cards evolved from tarot cards, which depicted vices, virtues and elemental forces and were employed for fortunetelling. In Fourteenth Century Italy they were called *Naib,* from the Hebrew *Naibi*, meaning "sorcery."

Tarot cards traditionally came in twenty-two card decks, twenty-one of which were numbered. The one unnumbered card was called *Le Mat*, a French word meaning "the fool." This tarot card was the father of today's Joker card in a deck of playing cards. The word "fool" comes from the Latin *follis*, meaning "a bag of wind." The Church looked both with favor and with fear upon tarot cards. In time they fell from the Church's grace and were banned in various parts of Europe in the late Fourteenth and mid-Fifteenth Centuries. Playing and tarot cards were called "the Devil's books" by Puritans and "the Devil's breviary" by others since they were thought to display the mysteries of evil. With the passing of the age of superstition, playing cards were no longer viewed as diabolic, and it was not considered sinful to play cards in good Christian homes.

Today we play with cards and we also exchange cards. At the holiday seasons and numerous other special occasions, we exchange not playing cards but greeting cards. Looking at the selections offered in a card shop, one wonders how many creative designers must be employed to provide such variety. There is, however, one greeting card that you will not likely find in any card shop or catalog. I'm suspicious that the reason you will never see this card is that it would never sell!

The card I'm referring to is a "Thank You" card, appropriate for Thanksgiving or for any time someone wanted to express gratitude. On the front of the card, along with some art, would be the words *I AM YOUR SERVANT*. Opening the card, the inside text would read *YOUR GIFT WAS BEAUTIFUL. CALL ON ME AT ANY TIME. I AM EAGER TO REPAY YOUR KINDNESS*.

I suspect that you're saying to yourself something like, "What a weird 'Thank You' card! To whom would I want to send it, other than someone in the Mafia?" Well, it would have been an ideal card to send to Jesus of Nazareth—or to anyone whose name appears in the Gospels. People of that time and place would have considered your card to be not only logical but the best of all expressions of gratitude! They certainly would have looked upon one of our typical "Thank You" cards as a Dead End note!

One of the first cultural rituals that we learned from our parents as small children was to say, "Thank you." When Aunt Julie gave us a piece of candy, our mother asked us *the* question, "Now what do you say to Aunt Julie?" What we really wanted to say was, "Got any more?" However, the hunger for our parents' approval and love (or the fear of their reproving) was stronger than the hunger for another piece of candy, so we gave the appropriate response. It may come as a surprise, but it's not likely that Jesus' mother ever taught him to say, "Thank you" for a gift.

Scripture scholar Dr. John Pilch points out that our culture's common expression, "Thank you," was rare in the Near Eastern and Mediterranean civilization at the time of Jesus. While the concept of *giving thanks* is common in Scripture, our polite verbal response to a gift was not. In the culture of Jesus, every gift implied a return gift. True gratitude was expressed by repaying the favor. The understood arrangement was, "You did me a favor; I do you a favor. Now you owe me another favor—and so on." Dr. Pilch writes:

> In Mediterranean culture, saying, "Thank you" effectively says, "I will never need you again, so let me terminate this relationship now by saying, 'Thank you' "…a risky venture in a world where centralized government did not work to the advantage of the peasants who never knew when they would need a favor again…. A common Middle Eastern saying asserts, "Don't thank me; you will repay me."

In St. Matthew's Gospel when Peter's mother-in-law was healed by Jesus, she did not send him a Hallmark "Thank You" card! Her fever miraculously gone, she instead got up from her sick bed and fixed supper for Jesus and his friends! To some of us Peter's mother-in-law's response might appear to be an example of male oppression. It's actually a Near Eastern expression of gratitude. Yet at the moment Jesus stood up from her supper table, he owed Peter's mother-in-law another favor! One wonders how he repaid her? Such an endless cycle of being obligated to others is not very attractive to us rugged individualist Americans with our heritage of independence. It should, however, make us rethink our cultural assumptions.

Our society's norms require that we respond to all gifts with an expression of gratitude, written or spoken. However, if we wish, we can become bi-cultural and express our gratitude Mafia-style! That group still retains the repayment concept of its ancient Mediterranean heritage. It was similar to the *I'll scratch your back, you scratch mine* system of the Irish political machines in Boston, New York, Kansas City, Chicago and other cities with large immigrant populations.

The next time someone does you a favor, instead of just sending a "Thank You" note, you might begin looking for opportunities to repay the favor with a favor. Daily life could be an endless cycle of giving and receiving, of being indebted and paying back the debt. When we live bi-culturally, we say, "Thank you"—as is our custom—but also, faithful to an older tradition, we are eager to repay the favor. As independence-loving Americans, the idea of remaining obligated to another person can fit about as comfortably as a medieval hair shirt! We dislike the "feel" of being indebted to others. Our preference is to respond to a gift with a clear-cut, obligation ending "Thank You" and not with an I.O.U. note or card.

Jesus called his original disciples beyond their culture when he said,

"When you give a lunch or dinner, do not invite your friends, relatives or wealthy neighbors. They might invite you in return and thus repay you. No, when you have a reception, invite the beggars and the crippled, the lame and the blind. You should be pleased that they cannot repay you, for you will be repaid in the resurrection of the just" (Lk. 14: 12-14). Our custom is to give gifts to people who in turn give gifts back to us. Jesus expands our boundaries of gift-giving by inviting us to observe a Mafia-style gratitude.

The "Mafia gratitude" we're called to practice is what happens when we've been awakened to how gifted we are—and, thus, how indebted! We have been blessed in countless ways: by God, by others

I AM YOUR SERVANT

and by good fortune. When we are truly aware of that, our sense of gratitude is heightened. To be truly grateful is to be indebted, to be eager to find ways to return the favors. To be truly grateful is reflected in our "back scratching" gift exchanging with family and friends.

Jesus also challenges each of us to be equally eager in being generous with those who *cannot* give us a gift in return! Yet giving to the poor can also be part of the Old World ritual of "You do me a favor, I'll do you one," since it provides us a way to repay God! When we truly believe that Christ lives in each person, that God dwells in each of us, then it's easy to return gifts to God for what we've been given. If you're grateful for your clean, warm bed, then give God—present in a homeless man—a gift of a warm bed on a cold night. If you are thankful for the twin gifts of your hands, then repay God—present in a poor woman—with an I.O.U. gift of a new pair of warm gloves. This endless cycle of gift giving is a Way of life, a Merry, Mafioso & Mystical Spirituality.

Be aware, however, that it's easy to be a cheapskate—or a closet cheapskate. It's easy to pretentiously pride oneself in being a disciple of Christ and yet be reluctant to give to others—unless some kind of

return is assured! How easily do we forget those who were generous with us in the past: parents, teachers, neighbors and friends. Oh, we were not rude; we thanked them! Our society's customs allow us to think that the score has been settled. Our desire not to be indebted to anyone blinds us to one of life's greatest realities.

We live our entire lives deeply indebted to God, to parents, teachers and count-less others we aren't even aware of! We are always indebted to anyone on life's journey who has loved us! Recall the key quote from *The Little Prince*: "You are responsible for those you love!" Love and friendship create that delightful Debtor's Prison from which no one who knows what makes the world go round ever escapes—or even wants to! Love is the greatest of all gifts and creates a debt that's impossible to repay. It is, however, a debt that provides great delight in the attempt to repay it.

Emotionally healthy parents do not burden their children with a sense of being indebted to them. The only payment they seek is for their children—once *they* become parents—to be the best parents they can be! The same kind of "passing on the gift" is the best way for any of us to repay teachers, mentors, life's various guides—like uncles, aunts or the coach who took a special interest in you—or even someone who once helped you when your car broke down.

Whenever you give something away, whether your time, energy, money or a gift, do it as you say, *"Ciao"* (pronounced chow). *Ciao*, used throughout the world both as a greeting and a farewell, comes from the dialect of Veneto in Northeast Italy. The people of that district, once ruled by Venice, practiced the custom of greeting and saying good-bye with the respectful phrase, *Schiavo vostro*, meaning "I am your slave." In the dialect of Veneto, the first word was pronounced "s-chow" and the phrase was eventually shortened to *ciao*.

Do you want to die a happy death? Then practice saying, *"Ciao"* and playing your Joker Thank You cards. Both at home and when you're out, fill your pockets with Joker I.O.U. cards and live as if in your lifetime you had given away so many I.O.U.'s that you couldn't even remember to whom you gave them all. Be eager at every turn to pay back those favors by treating all people as if *they each* had one of your I.O.U.'s in their pockets. If you do that, when it's your time to depart from this life, you can do so in peace because this old world will be a better place for your having been here! If you play the game of life with your hands full of holy Joker I.O.U.

cards, you will not only become aware of your royal divine inheritance, you can also die happy and at peace because you will be truly free of debt!

Prayerful Reflection
on the cycle of life's gifts:

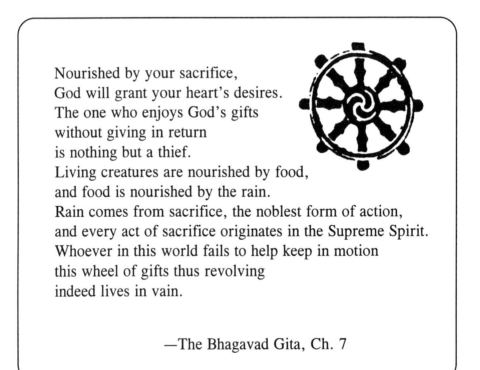

Nourished by your sacrifice,
God will grant your heart's desires.
The one who enjoys God's gifts
without giving in return
is nothing but a thief.
Living creatures are nourished by food,
and food is nourished by the rain.
Rain comes from sacrifice, the noblest form of action,
and every act of sacrifice originates in the Supreme Spirit.
Whoever in this world fails to help keep in motion
this wheel of gifts thus revolving
indeed lives in vain.

—The Bhagavad Gita, Ch. 7

Exercise:

WHY MUST MEDITATION BE SO SOLEMN?

Have you ever noticed how people in centering prayer or meditation seem to look so serious? If you didn't know that they were praying, you might think they were attending a funeral or a wake!

Put a bit of holy humor in your prayer by letting a slight smile come to your face as you lift your eyes and heart heavenward and as you and God are one in silent prayer. As the Psalmist (*pictured at left*) said, "Be still and know that I am God," to which we might add, "a happy, if not jolly, God!"

A smiling meditation will very naturally lead to a day in which that expression remains on your face, regardless of your ups and downs, enabling you to send countless holy joker cards in the mail .

INVENTORY
REDUCTION SALE

The opportunity of a lifetime!

Now you too can own your very own personal hermitage. Because of a decline in vocations, the religious order of the Holy Hermits St. Bridget and St. Brendan has been forced to disband. Fifty excellent hermitages of this former religious community are now available to the public at sensationally low prices!

Now you too can have a hermitage in your back yard or on the roof of your apartment building.

These used hermitages are the perfect solution to getting away from the constant noise and pressure of modern life. Ideal for a place of prayer, an oasis of peace or a quiet hideaway for creative reflection.

Playing Hide and Seek

Unless **you enjoy practical jokes,** I wouldn't call that 800 number or write to O'Brien's if I were you. To have your own personal hermitage is tempting, however, a place of solitude like the one that appears in the advertisement on the previous page. It would be a luxury indeed to have your own hideout where you could escape and get your wits together. Furthermore, a personal hermitage would make it easier to offer prayer, the basic act of any God-lover.

At times, perhaps, all of us have longed for a place where we could retreat to think and find some peace in the midst of our hectic lives. To do that, however, you needn't buy a used hermitage from the recently defunct order of St. Bridget and St. Brendan. You can have your very own hermitage, and it won't cost you a dime. Yet, it isn't free!

Every disciple of Jesus needs a hermitage. Jesus himself found such a space necessary in his life. It's highly unlikely that he had an actual cabin, but we do know that he slipped away from the busy domestic life of Nazareth, from the busy demands of his work, his ministry, to be alone with God. He even had a "hermitage" when he visited Jerusalem! In Luke's Gospel, after the Last Supper, Jesus went to pray. We are told, "Then he went out and made his way, *as was his custom*, to the Mount of Olives" (Lk. 22: 39).

Jesus, the layman, sought out places where he could hear the voice of God, so often drowned out by the shouts of the marketplace and normal household hustle and bustle. When asked about prayer, Jesus shared a secret about his private hermitage: "When you pray, go into your closet, close the door, and pray to your Father in private" (Mt. 6: 6). Now, the homes of poor Palestinians didn't often have closets or private rooms as our homes do. Jesus' listeners, however, knew that their hearts were the "closets," the private rooms of prayer.

Each of us has such a hermitage, and those who wish to make progress on the spiritual path enter that hidden hermitage daily. It is strange that a hideout so near to us is so difficult to find. It is so well hidden that few discover it. Those who do find it, however, are more than lucky, they are truly blessed. In his statement about prayer Jesus implied that when we visit such private places, we hear the quiet voice of God.

Jesus described himself as the Good Shepherd, an everyday image to his listeners. From that common knowledge he drew examples of the quality of intimacy between a loving shepherd and his sheep. Jesus said that his sheep hear his voice as he calls them each by name. It was commonplace for a shepherd to have pet names for his sheep, names based on distinctive colors, sizes, shapes and behavior patterns. Sheep of one flock feeding with those of another would recognize the voice of their shepherd and gather around him when called. In the same way, Jesus' disciples followed him because they recognized his voice.

Do you wonder what nickname or "pet" name Christ has for you? For many of us it could be "Sleepy," like one of the Seven Dwarfs in *Snow White*! For most of us meditation at the early hour of 6 a.m. would be considered a good one if we could simply stay awake! Yet, even if we manage to stay awake, I wonder how awake we truly are, how conscious of what we are doing and who we are. It seems that most of us spend our lives more or less asleep, sleep-walking during the day and sleep-resting during the night!

A hermitage is a wake-up house. Separated from the normal concerns that occupy us, we are able to awaken to our real work in life. Even if, like Mother Theresa of Calcutta, we are privileged to have a sacred lifework, we need to be awake to what we are doing. As Buddha said, "However much you may be engaged in activities for the good of others, do not neglect your own true purpose. Having clearly discerned your own true work, apply yourself to that work with diligence." Those could just as easily have been the words of Jesus, for his primary work was his relationship with God. While he was involved in caring for the needs of others, he did not neglect regularly retreating to his hermitage, to take time to withdraw into solitude with his Beloved.

A hermitage is a God-house where we go to be alone, to be intimate with God. As Jesus said, our heart is the hidden hermitage in which to encounter God. The scriptures of India express a similar teaching:

> In the center of the castle of God, our own body, there is a small shrine in the form of a lotus-flower, and within can be found a small space. We should find who dwells there, and we should want to know that One. And if anyone asks about the One who dwells in that small shrine, we can say: "The little space within the heart is as great as this vast universe. The heavens and the earth are there, and the sun and the moon and the stars; fire and lightning and winds are there; and all that now is and all that is not: for the whole universe is in that One and that One dwells within our heart."…When by the grace of God, one sees the glory of God within, then one sees God beyond the world of desire and all sorrows are left behind.
>
> —*Chandogya Upanishad*

Such an awakening does not prevent pain and suffering from happening in life, but it does teach us how to keep those experiences from becoming the baggage of life we drag behind wherever we go.

A hermitage is also a lookout tower. Within it we are able to see the trials, desires and events of life in their proper proportions. Distance always gives a purity and clarity of vision. Any disagreement or argument viewed "up close" is seen with distorted vision. We can see it as an island, isolated from the whole picture, separate from the fidelity, kindness, love and generosity of the offending person. The best way to miraculously recover our peace and perspective is to withdraw for a time within our lookout tower.

The Upanishads said, "When by the grace of God, one sees the glory of God...." That is the answer to the problem of finding the path to the heart-hermitage. We find it "by the grace of God"!

It's a short journey, but not an easy one, to that inner sanctuary. It requires the grace of God, the gift of prayer and the desire to be alone with "the One who lives in the shrine of the heart."

If you want to find the path that leads to your heart, it does truly help to create a special environment for the expedition. That "holy ground" doesn't have to be a wooden cabin left over from a defunct religious order or a mountain cave. It could be a bedroom, garage, basement or even a bathroom (which the British call a water *closet*). We all need a private place where we can be alone, separate from others. If possible, especially in the beginning of our practice, it should be a *quiet* place. God rarely shouts but is wont to speak in a quiet, intimate way.

After we have found a spot free of external noise, it helps to gently quiet the noise of the body, letting its tensions and numerous voices come to a rest. This can happen by engaging in a few minutes of deep, calm breathing. With each exhaling breath we can release thoughts, feelings and the demands of our work so they can flow out from us. With each breath we inhale, we can fill ourselves with peace and life.

We are not machines. We cannot push a button marked "Prayer" and instantly ride an elevator down to the hermitage of the heart. Yet, with our eyes closed, with reverence for both body and mind, we can gently descend into our hearts (keep in mind that if, like Alice, we can follow the white rabbit down the shaft into Wonderland, we must be prepared to meet the Mad Hatter and perhaps a whole deck of other holy jokers). This spiritual expedition is like finding our way through a darkened house, as we slowly move without sight, feeling our way rather than seeing. With each journey, however, the path to the heart-hermitage is more easily and quickly found.

Quiet of body, we quiet the mind, a true workaholic which is constantly busy about so many things in the past and the future. Like Elijah in his cave hideout, once we have passed beyond the noisy earthquakes and violent storms, we can begin to hear that tiny, whispering Voice which calls each of us by name.

If, by the grace of God, we are able to visit our heart-hermitage daily, we will be able to find our way to it when we are in great need. In the crisis moments of life, when we find ourselves trapped in a raging furnace of anger, in the torture chamber of envy or are lost in the swamp of self-pity, we will hear the voice of Christ calling us by name and leading us safely home. If we have been faithful in daily visits to our heart-hermitage, we will more easily find the path in troubled times, even if we are in the midst of a chatting crowd or bombarded by attacks of mind-noise from within.

Jesus knew that we are all closet mystics, if only we can find the right closet. Our visits to it are not a way to escape the world. On the contrary, the purpose of our retreats from the daily world is to truly discover the world! Those who make such spiritual expeditions find a world on the edge of glory, "the glory of God" mentioned in the Upanishads. For closet mystics, as Esther de Waal says, "the mundane is the edge of glory." For Monday Mystics, the commonplace becomes gloriously extraordinary. Yet, mindful of a saying from the tradition of the Desert Fathers, "Seek God, and not where God lives," we seek God, not only in sacred places but in *every* place.

Today in Kerry, in the southwest of Ireland, a country known for its rich history of hermits and hermitages, there's a folk expression, "Heaven is only a foot and a half above the height of a man." But the truth is that heaven is only a foot and a half below the height of each of us: in our hearts.

How easily we forget that our world is saturated with the sacred, that "the mundane is the edge of glory"! Our God is often a hidden God, and we wander through life easily missing the Divine Presence unless we take time to visit our "wake-up houses." Since our days are usually crowded with commitments, the cost of waking up will not be cheap. We will have to create time for visits to our hermitages. We must also be careful to go for the right reasons. Those holy hideouts should not be there to hide from something or someone, but paradoxically to *find* something, to find Someone.

Most of us had a hideout as a child. Whether it is under the front porch, in the attic of the garage, a tree house or a favorite place in a field near home, a childhood hideout is a special, numinous place. When you go in search of the hermitage of the heart, that hideout where you can be alone with God, you capture an adventure which, like Alice's, no child ever outgrows.

This reflection concludes with a story about a Jewish rabbi and his son. One day the young boy came into the house after a game of hide-and-seek, with tears streaming down his face. The father took the child into his arms and asked what was wrong. The child tearfully explained that he and the other children had been playing hide-and-seek and that he had hidden himself, but no one had come seeking him. The father kissed his small son lovingly and said, "My child, now you know how God feels. For God is hidden in our midst and waits patiently for us to begin the search."

Exercise:

BLEST ARE THOSE WHO LIVE FULLY AWAKE

Jesus listed among the holy, the blessed, those who are pure or single of heart. To be "single-hearted" requires that only one thing, which embodies our desire for God, occupies our consciousness. It means that a single thing at a time fills our heart and attention. Jesus promised that those who lived in such a state would not only be blessed but would, indeed, see God! We tend to think of mystics as people who have visions of God. While you might hesitate to call yourself a *mystic,* if you are able to be totally absorbed in some action, you should recall Thomas Merton's words. He said that mystics are not those who see different, even divine things, but rather those who see differently! To be awake, aware and mindful is the key to seeing life in a different and sacred way.

So, when you spend time in your hermitage, practice doing everything simply. Do one thing at a time–whether praying, sitting, reading or eating. Do it wakefully, attending all the time to the Presence, listening carefully for the quiet Voice.

Zombies and Zanies

Early **Franciscans decorated** the hoods on their cloaks with asses' ears and bells to look like professional fools. These early followers of St. Francis called themselves *Mundi Moriones*, meaning "Fools of the World." By making themselves appear as laughable buffoons, they were taking the words of Jesus at face value. Wearing asses' ears also implied a belief that primitive humans emerged from beasts. Having asses' ears on their hoods said that the "beast" still lurks within us. Humans can easily treat each other like beasts of burden—as Claivius Narcisse once discovered.

The bells of jesters worn by Franciscans also alluded to lepers who were called the "living dead." Lepers used a bell to warn anyone approaching, while calling out, "Unclean, unclean." Poor Claivius Narcisse found himself among another kind of living dead in 1962 on the island of Haiti. He suddenly became sick and was taken to a local hospital. Upon being admitted, he told the doctor that it felt like his heart was slowing down. Although his stomach seemed to be on fire, the rest of his body felt like it was freezing to death. He died a few hours later and was buried, the cause of death never determined. However, eighteen years after his death, Claivius reappeared in his village in Haiti, quite alive! He told his astonished friends that, although unable to speak or move, he was conscious as the doctor told his sister that he was dead. He was a witness to his own funeral, even to the reality of dirt being shoveled on top of his coffin. All the while he was unable to do anything about it. The next thing Claivius remembered, he was standing in a kind of trance next to his own grave site, watching two men refilling the grave. They then tied a rope around his hands and took him to a farm where for the next eighteen years he labored as a field slave! Daily he was given a dose of something to drink, but one day the farm boss forgot to administer the drug and Claivius was able to escape. He separated from the other zombie field workers and joyfully returned to his family who had mourned his death so many years before.

Is this zombie story factual, or is it the kind of front page story you would expect to find on the cover of the *National Enquirer*? If you believe in voodoo and in the power of houngans, voodoo priests and priestesses, then you'll acknowledge how it can be true. According to Dr. Lamarque Douyon, the director of the Psychiatric Center in Port-au-Prince, Haiti, zombies and zanies are not the result of voodoo power. They are, rather, people who have been *drugged* by a voodoo sorcerer. They are pronounced dead and are buried. Later they are dug up from their graves and kept drugged during their enslavement as agricultural workers. In his book *Man, Myth & Magic* Richard Cavendish gives an account of a parish priest's interview in 1959 with a zombie field worker who wandered into a village in Haiti. When he was taken to the local police station, it was reported that they gave him a glass of saltwater which cleared his memory. Awakened from his drugged state, he gave the police his name and information about others, likewise drugged, with whom he had been forced to work.

Zombies, in case you should encounter one, are easily recognizable. Their arms dangle lifelessly at their sides; their skin is pale and lifeless (they do not sweat). The most striking feature is their gaze. They stare straight ahead, eyes dulled and unfocused. Zombies do not acknowledge the presence of others. They go about their tasks without awareness, as if they were mechanical robots. While this is a description of zombies, it often fits the average modern consumer! Haven't you seen shopping malls or stores crowded with people who have blank, expressionless eyes, walking around like robots without any recognition of those around them. Especially at times of sales and around the holidays, these consumer zombies seem to be programed by one single message: "Get the gift, get the gift, get the gift."

The stress produced by the complexity of modern life can turn us into mechanical men and women. It can make us dull of eye and solely intent upon accomplishing our tasks, not unlike zombies, the "walking dead." We easily become like those creatures who hibernate, who have the ability to lower their body thermostats from 98 to about 55 degrees. They find a hole in a hollow tree or some cave and become the "living dead." We can also shut down and curl up in a cave of self-absorption. As certain voodoo drugs can create zombies, so the powerful Too-Much-To-Do-In-Too-Short-A-Time condition can easily drug you and me. Aware of this, let us be watchful and careful.

Houngans, voodoo priests, draw strange signs with cornmeal flour on the earthen floor of courtyards or temples as a preparation for their rituals. If you happen to be present, it would be prudent to not look at those strange designs for they can entrap your mind and heart. The houngans of Madison Avenue—you can substitute the name of your main shopping street—also weave spellbinding designs, not out of cornmeal flour but with neon and four-color advertisements. Their mesmerizing voodoo power can easily turn your gaze only upon yourself and your desires. The same voodoo magic can hover over the agenda you've drawn up for your day. That list of so many things to do in such a short time can turn you into a zombie-like robot intent upon nothing but the completion of your list. The result is a temporary blindness to the presence of others and their needs or to the beauty of the day and your surroundings.

If you feel like a drugged zombie and see scary symptoms in yourself which indicate that you may be one of the "walking dead"— and you want to escape—here's one way. Take your long list of things to purchase or your busy agenda of tasks you MUST accomplish at work today and tear it in half! With only half of those things to do, the most essential ones, you will be free to respond in a human and holy way to all that you encounter. You will be free to respond with love and attention to those you meet or those with whom you live and work. Trust me, tearing that list in half and focusing only on what is really necessary for today has a magical power to make you awake and free.

The ageless song of the Gospels is, "Awake, rise from your drugged sleep and watch out for the houngans!" The ongoing challenge Jesus presented to those who wish to be his disciples: "Stay Awake! Do not be caught napping! Be watchful!" (See Mt. 24: 4, 42). The work of those who take the spiritual path seriously, who seek to be holy, is liberation from zombieism. "Wake up" is a personal call to keep from being counted among the "walking dead," to reject living like a robot.

Perhaps your response to such a wake-up call might be, "I have too many responsibilities to practice such wake-up exercises; there's just too much for me to do." Ah, paradoxically hidden in that excuse is the secret of success. Your busiest times are ideal times to integrate your prayer and spiritual exercises into daily life. Such times are anti-hibernation times. They are times to translate your meditation and personal prayer into living—shopping, baking, traveling, working and having fun—that is fully awake. Regardless of how devout your prayer is, how exquisitely still and free from distractions your meditation may be, what good is a spiritual practice if it doesn't free you from being a spiritual zombie? Religious exercises can even drug you into a zombie-like state in which your only concern is *your* enlightenment or saving *your* soul. Beware of all religious exercises that become holy houngans with the power to make you dull of eye, blind to the needs or even the presence of others. Spiritual zombies can be just as self-absorbed in their religious tasks as shopping mall zombies.

One simple but not easy saltwater cure (remember, that's one of the ways to wake up a zombie) for going through life as a human robot, on automatic pilot, is to make every action count. We have developed the habit of being only partially present to routine actions, since they seem so boring. Since we seem forever short of time, we habitually piggyback routine actions, thinking about "important" things while performing automatic actions. To make every action count means striving to be as fully conscious as possible to both routine and more challenging daily activities. This cure sounds so simple, yet it is most difficult. The reason is that the most dreaded houngan, the one with the greatest power to make you into a zombie, is your mind.

If you think you're busy, think about your poor mind. It's perpetually busy with your problems, regrets, worries and plans for tomorrow. Try saying to your mind, "This morning I only want to be conscious of the action of dressing: which arm I put through the sleeve first, the feel of the texture of my sweater, which shoe I slip on first, how it fits on my foot." Think that way, however, and be prepared for a problem. Your mind may shout back, "I've got more important things to consider. Are you out of your mind? Why should I waste my time thinking about such dull, meaningless things?" Or perhaps when you give your mind the task of doing any routine action mindfully, it will smile and say, "Of course, that's a wonderful idea, how religious and what a good discipline." Then after about twenty seconds it will use its voodoo magic and switch all channels to something juicy for you to worry about, fear or regret. Despite the capacity of the mind for trickery, persevering in this one daily assignment—to be as conscious as possible in everything you do—is excellent saltwater work.

Another saltwater cure is a kind of reverse voodoo doll ritual. Black voodoo places pins in a doll which represents another person to bring about harmful and deadly designs upon that person. Whenever you catch yourself in the zombie state of a drugged field worker—regardless of the kind of work you're doing— pinch yourself. Just as you might pinch yourself if you feel yourself falling asleep while driving, you can give your- self a wake-up pinch to make you mindful of what you are doing at the present moment. Mindfulness is one of the key concepts in all the great religious traditions because God is present only in the eternal present moment! The human mind, however, often finds the present moment boring and so is eager to escape to the past or future time zones.

All of us are wont to look for some mystical encounter, a magical word or easy formula for achieving holiness. Most of us have tried prayer, meditation and the other traditional methods, but we don't seem any closer today to holiness than we were years ago. We've tried to be mindful but have found it too difficult to sustain. We attend conferences and presentations on prayer, make retreats with Eastern spiritual masters, read books on Tibetan mysticism, all with the hope that something will bring us the magic of spiritual success.

The paradox is that the answer has been right in front of us all the time, and it's so simple. The secret to success is found in two words: "Wake Up!" It's nothing new; in fact, it is one of the oldest of all spiritual challenges. All of our practices may aid us in waking up, but there is no once and forever formula. It inevitably comes back to "praying always," to a continuous "practice of the presence of God," to a constant mindfulness, to a daily discipline of waking up. Jesus said that his disciples were to be the "salt of the earth." This saying has many implications, but this reflection on zombies, about living only half-conscious lives, suggests another meaning.

When you have struggled to be as awake as possible to each action in your life, rejoice because you have become part of a worldwide salt-water cure. As you go about your many daily tasks, regardless of how busy you are, sprinkle a little salt on your smile and give it away. Whenever you come face to face with a stressed-out co-worker, a hassled store clerk, a robot-like shopper or anyone with dull, zombie eyes, remember that you have the magical power to help cure their hibernation, their unconscious withdrawal from life. Look the person straight in the eye with as much love as possible and invest your "thank you" or request with overflowing kindness and sincerity. You may be surprised at the power of your magic as you watch that person—even if only for a minute or two—wake up!

Exercises:

WAYS TO LIVE MINDFULLY

Speed is the enemy of mindfulness. An excellent exercise to increase your capacity to be mindful involves slowing down your perform-ance of some selected action. You can choose one or two common activities you perform during the day and carry them out as deliber-ately and mindfully as you can. Such slowing down allows you to focus your attention fully upon what you are doing at the moment. Practice this for a brief time with your total attention. You will likely, however, need to learn to be patient with yourself since your habit of inattentiveness has been formed by many years of differing degrees of absent-mindedness. Consider the three or four minutes in which you exercise a fullness of attention to be a time of prayer. The ability to live most of your life mindfully will be achieved gradually and only by winning daily small, seemingly insignificant victories.

AN INATTENTIVE ALARM SIGNAL

Because fire can easily trap us while asleep or busy, almost all homes today have smoke alarms that give an early alert and awaken us to danger. These alarms usually require batteries and need to be frequently inspected to see if they're operating correctly. You have many commonplace experiences in your daily life which act as Zombie Alarms that require no batteries but only a smiling recognition. Take only ten seconds for a brief prayer the next time you find yourself asking, "Now where did I put the car keys?" or "Where did I leave my eyeglasses?" That kind of question is a signal that you have been sleepwalking, inattentive to what you are doing. Whenever you ask yourself this kind of "alarm" question, be thankful that you have a chance to be awakened. Be grateful for the opportunity to say a mini-prayer like, "O God, help me to live fully awake to my every deed and thought." A cousin to this Zombie Alarm exercise is the practice of verbalizing routine actions: "Now I am placing my car keys on the book shelf." If done with a prayerful inner attitude, both can help you achieve great mindfulness.

Wundersucht

F **olly in all forms** thrives in times of great change and transition. This is especially true at transition times in the year. Whenever time has moved from the old to the new, foolishness has flourished. New Year's, Shrove Tuesday before Ash Wednesday and the Feast of Fools in spring traditionally have been folly times when daily patterns are upset by ordinary people acting foolishly. By mutual social consent people engage in folly by changing sex roles, turning hierarchies upside down and violating other ancient taboos.

The past hundred years has seen a hunger for respectability sweeping over the middle classes, replacing with the starch of seriousness our natural appetite for the silly. The Industrial Age and the assembly line had no place for the clown or jester. Further, respectability, the need to be taken seriously, has robbed us of the natural flow of folly and the magical play that once marked the transitional crossing points of each year and of each individual's life.

The circus has practically become a relic, the traveling magician and P.T. Barnum's Wonders of the World but a faint memory. Yet those whose lives are dull routines still hunger for the wondrous, as do those beset by crisis and radical change. Many today feel this hunger, not unlike those who lived long ago in Templemore, Ireland.

The year was 1920, and violence was the order of the day in Ireland. The British government had outlawed the Irish nationalist movement, and in response the nationalists launched a bloody guerrilla war against the Black and Tan English troops sent to restore order. On August 15, the feast of the Assumption of Mary, the town hall and several other buildings in Templemore, located in county Tipperary, were burned to the ground. Six days later all the religious statues and pictures in the home of Thomas Dwan and his sister-in-law, Mrs. Maher, began simultaneously to bleed!

News spread quickly, attracting an initial trickle of pilgrims to Templemore. Soon, however, excursion trains from Dublin were rolling into town. The Thomas Cook Travel Agency inquired as to whether the small inns in the town could accommodate two thousand pilgrims at a time. Those eager to see the weeping images came from as far away as America and even from India and Japan. It was estimated by authorities that by the time the statues had stopped bleeding, about one month after they began, close to one million people had visited the town of Templemore.

On March 30, 1919, in the small village of Limpias in northern Spain, a twelve-year-old girl was praying before a large carved wooden crucifix when she saw the eyes move. She told her parish priest about her experience, but when he came he could see nothing unusual in the crucifix. Soon other villagers heard about what had happened and came to the church. Some also saw the eyes moving, while for others it appeared that Christ's face and neck were wet with sweat. A whirlwind of excitement filled the little village, but for two weeks nothing happened to drastically change life there. For his part, the parish priest made no comment one way or the other about the series of events.

However, by May 4 special trains were bringing throngs of

pilgrims to the village of Limpias to see the crucifix. As thousands crowded the streets, bells were rung and firecrackers lit; the excitement was intense. Now the manifestations became more and more startling. Many saw the figure on the cross looking at them, sometimes with kindness, at other times with sadness. Others saw drops of blood on the figure's body or the head moving from side to side. Still others heard sighs or whispers coming from the Christ figure. By now the number of pilgrims had grown to four thousand a day! Eventually, however, the manifestations ended, and the village of Limpias was forgotten.

These are only two of many documented cases of reported wonders and visions. Today, millions of pilgrims visit great shrines where Mary, the Blessed Mother, is said to have appeared: Lourdes in France, Fatima in Spain and Guadalupe, outside of Mexico City to name a few. To these traditional shrines have been added the more recently reported visitation at Medjugorje in former Yugoslavia and even one at Lubbock, Texas.

What has motivated millions who annually make pilgrimages to such towns as Templemore in Ireland or Lubbock in Texas? What attracts the thousands who fill outdoor stadiums to see faith healers?

There are many reasons, some of them mysterious, as to why pilgrims flock to places that report strange signs in the sky, miraculous cures and supernatural phenomena like weeping statues, why people leave home and work to seek out such marvels. But I wonder if one of the main reasons might not be *wundersucht*!

We all have a little *wundersucht* in us. A German word that means "a passion for miracles," this hunger is part of our collective fascination with magic. And religion and magic have long been bedmates and fellow travelers.

Religion is a code of morality and a system of beliefs which offers an explanation for life on earth, which gives a sense of meaning and purpose to existence. However, at the core of every religion, often just below the surface, is mysticism, the direct experience of God. Usually at least a thin veil keeps the natural and supernatural planes of existence separate. However, when it comes to miracles, they quickly fuse, whether the event is an appearance of the Blessed Virgin or a cripple cured by a faith healer in a revival tent. Such occurrences quickly bring us into contact with our passion for miracles.

We live in an age of *wundersucht*, for it is not restricted to the pious and religious. Motion pictures today draw millions to theaters with the promise of magical special effects. And the *Enquirer* relies on the millions hungry for the unusual when publishing such headlines, complete with photos, as "Woman Pregnant with Child by UFO Pilot!" Old P.T. Barnum also knew that we all have *wundersucht* in our blood and made a fortune by providing amazing attractions for people to see. Today there is also an aura around healing quartz crystals, pyramid power, ESP, channeling, designer drugs, Eastern gurus with supernatural powers, herbs that will cure whatever ails you and even the marvelous powers of computers and technology. It's all become big business for the millions of non-churched who are pilgrims of high-tech *wundersucht*. Madison Avenue advertisers know that if they want to sell a product, all they have to do is add one word to their promotion copy: "Magical"!

We all love the magical, and we have a passion for miracles, for cosmic magic. Miracles are God's magic, signs of power that make bread appear in the desert or cancer disappear in a sick pilgrim at a shrine. The idea of miracles being magic, even divine magic, might strike some people as cheapening or offensive. While most of us enjoy the marvels performed by a magician, we know that making something disappear or reappear is really only a trick. So if magic is a slight of hand, are miracles simply a slight of mind?

"A slight of mind?" you might ask. "Are you implying that miraculous cures and whirling suns in the sky are illusions created by the mind? What about the stigmata of St. Francis? His body bore the nail wounds of the body of Christ; they actually bled. That's hardly an illusion!" True, St. Francis and Padre Pio of contemporary times have borne in their bodies the wounds of the crucified Christ. Yet did you know that over one hundred Moslem mystics bore in their bodies the bleeding wounds of the Prophet Mohammed? Whatever we desire with enough passion can actually happen. If you become totally identified with a holy beloved, then indeed miraculous things can happen to you.

Among the lost stories from the childhood of Jesus is one that speaks of the miraculous:

One day, an eight-year-old Jesus ran to the door of his home and cried, "Mother, I'm going with the others to see a holy man who is passing through our village. They say he can turn stones into bread."

Mary called her son to her side and said, "Yeshua, I have something to say to you." Then she leaned over and whispered in Jesus' ear. He looked up at her with a startled gaze and then went and sat on their doorstep as the people rushed down the street in great haste to see the holy man.

Again, at the age of eleven, when Jesus went with his parents up to the Temple for a great feast, he said to Mary, "Mother, I am going over to the other courtyard for a while. They say that a prophet is teaching there. He can foretell the future and can make fire descend from the sky."

Mary responded, "Yeshua, have you forgotten what I taught you? Come here, my beloved." She leaned close to Jesus and whispered in his ear. Thereupon Jesus silently accompanied his mother to worship.

Perhaps we should pause in the midst of this lost story for a moment to recall Jesus' words about *wundersucht*, the passion for wondrous signs: "Unless you people see signs and wonders, you do not believe" (Jn. 4: 48). When the Pharisees and Sadducees asked him for some sign in the sky, he said, "An evil, faithless age is eager for a sign" (Mt. 16: 4). Remember too when Jesus was teaching one day and a woman called out, saying that his mother's womb and breast were wondrous and blessed, Jesus responded, "Rather, blest are they who hear the word of God and keep it" (Lk. 11: 27-28).

Recall also that the hometown folks of Jesus' village were upset by his claims about being the "bread that came down from heaven." They said, "Is this not Jesus, the son of Joseph? Do we not know his mother and father?" (Jn. 6: 41-42). What they were saying was, "How dare this man claim to be extraordinary when his parents are so ordinary! How dare he claim to be a living miracle!"

Yet, wasn't Jesus a miracle worker? Wasn't he the source of numerous cures and wonders that caused the crowds to pursue him? Yes, but to understand that, let's return to our unfinished story from the childhood of Jesus. Recall in the story that Jesus twice came to his mother burning with *wundersucht*, first when he was only eight years old and again when he was eleven.

> When Jesus was thirty, he went down to the Jordan Valley with others from his village to see the wild, hairy prophet of the desert, John the Baptist. Reports had arisen everywhere about this visionary, mostly from those who had experienced conversions in their lives. Jesus, like the others, went down into the waters to be baptized. As he rose out of the water, a voice (someone said it was a clap of thunder) said, "You are my beloved Son, upon you my favor rests" (Mk. 1: 11). Then the voice whispered something in the wet ear of Jesus. The crowd didn't hear it; John didn't even hear it; but Jesus did! The words were the same as his mother's, but this was the voice of God: "If you are hungry for miracles, then work them yourself!"

Jesus went off into the desert to ponder the strange message that both his mother and Heavenly Father had spoken to him, "If you are hungry for miracles, then work them yourself!" What God and Mary said to Jesus is also spoken deeply within us: "If you are afire with *wundersucht*, don't go on a pilgrimage to see a miracle, don't light a candle and pray for one; perform a miracle yourself. *You* do something wonder-full!" Yes, you have that God-given power within you!

When someone offends you, you can "miraculously" forgive that person on the spot! Or when you're busy and someone comes in and asks you for help, you can "miraculously" rise up from your task and with a broad smile come to that person's assistance! These are only two examples of many miracles that you can perform. Such were the ordinary miracles that Mary of Nazareth performed daily. And you and I can do even greater wonders!

The hunger for the magical and miraculous is part of being human, as all magicians know. That hunger is our common desire for *wundersucht*. There was a news story about a thirteen-year-old boy from Vietnam who had come to the United States. His family in Vietnam had arranged his passage to America through a welfare agency, telling him that he could make it possible for them to join him if he got a good education. He entered high school barely able to speak English, yet four years later he graduated *magna cum laude*, sixth in a class of 600! He lived alone in a poorly furnished room provided by welfare. He studied under a bare light bulb and often went hungry. When asked by a student counselor what he did when he had no money, he answered, "When I don't have money, I don't eat!" His high school counselor also told him that if he really wanted to be sure to get a college education, he should try for an athletic scholarship in addition to an academic one. So he joined the high school wrestling team. In his senior year he was named state wrestling champion! He did all these wondrous and impossible things because of his enormous desire to bring his family to America.

Such miracles of love happen in your life and mine, but they are usually commonplace miracles. How many pilgrims clustering in a crowd of thousands in hopes of seeing strange phenomena in the skies or rushing to see a weeping statue race blindly past a multitude of miracles that line every roadside? How is it that thousands are moved to great piety and prayer at the sight of a statue with weeping eyes and are not so moved by the sight of tears in the eyes of a mother whose son is addicted to drugs or a homeless man whose face is filled with sadness?

Millions travel vast distances to shrines and sites of great miracles because they believe that such places are God-filled. Jesus, however, said that the kingdom of heaven is all around us, that the presence of the Divine Mystery is here, wherever *here* is for you. If nothing miraculous ever happens where you are, is it because God has selected other geographic places to be present? Or if Mary, the mother of Jesus, were to appear to you, might she not say to you what she said to her son in our story: "If you are hungry for miracles, then make one yourself!"

If it seems to us that miracles and experiences of divine power are present only in certain isolated places on this small planet, is that more God's choice or ours? You and I who experience *wundersucht*, that passion for miracles, need to remember those parting and challenging words of Jesus to his disciples: "I solemnly assure you, the one who has faith in me will do these works that I do, and *greater* far than these" (Jn. 14: 12).

Exercise:

CREATING THE MIRACULOUS

If you wish to do the kind of works that Christ promised his disciples would do, how should you begin? One way to start might be to take an object that is found in every home, car and in many disciples' purses: a mirror.

The mother-word of both miracle and mirror is the Latin *mirari*, "to wonder at." In days long ago, to see an image of oneself in a piece of polished metal did indeed cause wonder. Mirrors were wonder-full things for ancient peoples, who could see their reflections only in pools of still water.

Who among us today is ever caught up in wonder when looking into the mirror while shaving or combing one's hair? Mirrors are usually only practical necessities for those who wish to be well-groomed and neat. However, your mirror can also become a rich instrument of inspiration for learning how to perform miraculous deeds.

Recall the famous scene with the evil queen in the fairy tale *Snow White*. She would stand in front of her mirror and ask, "Mirror, mirror on the wall, who's the fairest of them all?" A prayer exercise that I would like to suggest is a playful parallel to those words. Daily, after you have finished with the practical use of your mirror, stand for a moment in silence. Then look directly into your mirror and with great devotion pronounce this short prayer:

> Mirror, mirror on the wall,
> may I look with love on all.

Creating the Miraculous, Continued

When, as a holy fool, you have finished reciting your mini mirror prayer, consciously, as your day begins, look with eyes of love upon every tree, flower, animal, person and task of your day. Each time you find that you are tempted to think a careless thought of anger, criticism, resentment, indifference or of envy, remember your mirror prayer and open yourself to seeing the miraculous flashing out from all creation.

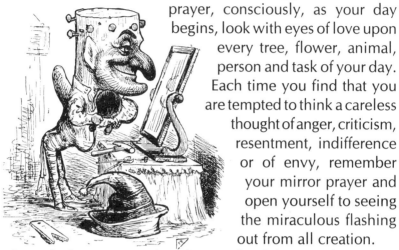

At such times remember the words of the Fourth Century saint, Jerome: "The face is the mirror of the mind, and eyes without speaking confess the secrets of the heart." If your heart hides darkness or indifference, your eyes will shout out those secrets. But praying with your mirror will not only keep you aware of all that is in your heart, it can help you change your thoughts and your inner attitudes. It can help you to expose to redeeming love all that is unworthy of a follower of the Lord of Love. You can also travel light years in transforming your heart by consciously beginning to look with love-filled eyes upon friend and enemy, stranger and alien.

Thus you can use the mirrors of your home, car or purse as sacred images to create the miraculous. They can become instruments of pardon for those who harm you, compassion for those who suffer and kindness toward the stranger. And like the mirrors that magnify your image, your new prayer can help you cultivate a love like that of Christ, large enough to embrace the whole world, great enough to die for all.

Turmoil at the Ballpark

Fan has "miraculous" apparitions

by O'Leary Brown,
Times Staff Reporter

The Blue Sox last place standing in the league has caused the giant 50,000 seat stadium to be nearly empty for the team's recent home games. Only a handful of faithful fans still turns out to see the Sox struggle during their recent losing streak which now has reached nine in a row and fifteen losses out of their last seventeen games. While the past weeks have seen the ball park nearly deserted, last night the huge parking lot was jammed to overflowing. For half a mile in all directions around the stadium the side streets were filled with vehicles. Cars, pickup trucks and large diesel tour-busses, many from out of state, clogged the surrounding streets. Throngs of people from all walks of life—black and white, rich and poor, as well as hundreds of handicapped in wheelchairs and walkers—crowded the stadium parking lot as they have for the last several Saturday nights. Many in the huge crowd, estimated by police at over 50,000, were carrying tambourines, while others carried cameras.

The presence of numerous TV news mobile units and camera crews added to the police department's crowd-control problem. Several large groups of Hell's Angels heightened the electricity in the air—as well as the apprehension—and complicated the traffic jams. The work of the police was surprisingly easy, however, since the mood of the massive crowd was light and festive, at times even solemn. The mass of people gathered shoulder-to-shoulder in the ballpark parking lot was not there to see the home team break their losing streak. They were there to catch a glimpse of the Virgin Mary! Each Saturday night more of the pious and curious have assembled in the hope that they too might see a vision of the Virgin Mary, the Mother of God.

The first apparition occurred three months ago, late one Saturday afternoon, to a Mr. Mickey Monroe of 807 North 18th Street. Mr. Monroe, a black automobile mechanic, had come to see a Blue Sox night game. He had arrived early and together with a few friends was enjoying a pre-game tailgate party on the back of his pickup truck. The miraculous event occurred, according to Mr. Monroe, after sunset, when the battery of tall field-lights had just lit up the western sky and a full moon was rising in the east. In a press interview in the parking lot, Mr. Monroe spoke of the apparition:

"Mr. Monroe, you say that you saw the Virgin Mary here in this parking lot. What actually did you see?"

"I saw the Blessed Virgin Mary. She appeared right over there. She was standin'...ah...more like floatin'... above a yellow '87 Buick. She looked like all the pictures of her that you've ever seen, except that in her right hand she had a tambourine. In fact, it was the sound of the tambourine that caused me to look up, and there she was, as I said, kinda' floatin' above the hood of that yellow Buick."

"Were there, Mr. Monroe, any other miraculous signs, like whirling suns and that sort of thing?"

"I didn't see anything like that, but other people here in the parking lot said that they saw the moon doing strange things."

"You're referring to the 'Yo–Yo Moon'?"

"Yeah. People said that the moon rolled up and down like it was a yo-yo. Some folks tried to take Polaroid pictures of it, but I guess because it was night—and with the glare of all those bright stadium lights—you can't see much in the snapshots."

"Mr. Monroe, are you a devout Catholic, and do you have a special devotion to the Mother of God?"

"That's what's strange. I'm not Catholic! I was raised a Baptist, and I've never even seen the inside of a Catholic church."

"That is unusual, isn't it? Don't visions of the Blessed Virgin usually appear only to Catholics? This must be some kind of a religious first!"

"I guess so. I don't know why the Lady appeared to me. Not only am I not Catholic, I haven't been to *any* church since I was a kid. I'm...ah...what you might call religiously uncommitted. I'm just an ordinary car mechanic who enjoys a good game of baseball."

"Mr. Monroe, just what was the message that the Virgin Mary gave you, a message you say is for the whole world?"

"Well, each time she's appeared— and that's about seven times now, always on Saturday evening after sunset—she's always said the same thing to me: 'Mickey, tell the people that God loves them all and that if the world is to be saved they must dance the polka!'"

"Mr. Monroe, that's a rather unusual heavenly message, isn't it? A message from God for people to dance the polka?"

"Like I said, I'm not Catholic. Maybe for them it ain't so strange. If I was church-goin', it probably would have been a real bummer. I mean, God callin' me, a Baptist, to save the world by dancin' the polka—or any kind of dancing!"

The press interview concluded with those remarks by Mr. Monroe who said it was time for the evening devotions to begin. As bright TV camera lights panned the parking lot, the crowd began doing the polka to the sounds of accordion music and tambourines. Elderly black-veiled nuns, black-jacketed Hell's Angels, little girls in white First Communion dresses, college students and middle-class couples from suburbia all joined hands as they joyfully danced the polka.

A Blue Sox fan fighting his way through the dancing throng was interviewed: "As a baseball fan, what do you think of all this?"

"Think about it? I *know* that it's insane—stupid! If these people want to pray, they should go to a church. This is a ballpark parking lot. What the hell are they doing here, blocking up the parking lot?"

"It's easy to see why you're disturbed, but apparitions of the Virgin Mary have been reported here. I guess she has chosen this parking lot as a religious shrine."

"I'm an American, and I believe in the separation of Church and Sports. Hell, I had to park half a mile from here tonight! There's no room in this parking lot—what with all these accordion players and religious fanatics filling the place. The next thing you know, they'll be edging their way into the ballpark itself!"

No statement on the apparitions has yet come from the local Catholic Archdiocese. The Cardinal remains unavailable for comment. A Church official, however, said that the Church had nothing to say about the "supposed" apparitions. He further stated that since Mary had appeared not to a Roman Catholic but to a Baptist, it seemed to be a matter for the Baptist Church. The Vatican likewise has refused any comment on the reported apparitions.

Father VanderVoo, a biblical scholar and professor at St. Mary's Seminary, said in a telephone interview that the apparitions could be seen as a fulfillment of the vision of Jeremiah, chapter thirty-one: "With age-old love I have loved you; so have I kept my mercy toward you. Again, I will restore you...O Virgin Israel; carrying your festive tambourines, you shall go forth dancing with the merrymakers."

A militant Catholic group, the Marian Blue Berets, was picketing and praying at the entrances of the parking lot. A spokesperson for the group said that the Berets have been demonstrating against these Polka

Pilgrimages because, in his words, "They're fake!" While the Pope and the Church have made no judgments about the supposed apparitions, the Blue Berets denounced them because the message of the Virgin has said nothing about praying the rosary.

Pastors of most local churches, however, both Catholic and non-Catholic, have taken a wait-and-see position. Many of those interviewed said that since the apparitions began they've noticed increased attendance at parish dances. "Anything," said one local parish priest who requested that his name not be used, "that calls people back to prayer and God can't be all bad."

The Story Gets Exciting

I laid the book in my lap and closed my eyes. The last entry, the newspaper article about the appearance of the Blessed Virgin, seemed out of place in the handbook. Or did it hold some truth that only a parable could address? I had been so caught up in reading *HOLY FOOLS* that hours had slipped away.

I heard them before I saw them! From down the road, below a hill, came loud shouts of angry threats and violent expressions of outrage exploding like bombs. A crowd of townsfolk were running toward me up the forest road from the village. Some were carrying heavy sticks and clubs. Others clutched rocks like hand grenades. Leading the angry mob was a black-robed priest and what appeared to be a rotund nun with a crosier.

When they reached me, the priest, puffing and out of breath, demanded, "Have you seen him?"

Before I could ask whom they were seeking, others in the crowd began shouting, "Did that heretic come this way?" and, "Where's that filthy idiot who..." and "Disgraceful, shameful it was!"

The priest held up his lily-white hand, "Quiet, fools, we're losing time. Young man, have you see a white-bearded man in his early sixties come this way? When he escaped from us, he was seen running up this road into the forest."

"No, Father, I haven't seen anyone. No one has passed this way in hours." To myself, I thought, "Oh, I fear it's the master they're after. What could he have done to upset them so?" Several of the men were clutching their clubs with such vehemence that I was afraid to confess that I was a disciple of the man they were seeking.

"Why are you looking for this man?" I asked. "What did he do to anger you?"

"What did he do?" bellowed the fat nun in full black religious habit, her veil swirling about her head as if she were wearing a thunderstorm cloud, "He should be castrated for that lewd...." Turning to the priest, she continued, "And, Father, I was shocked when he accused you of 'Incense!'"

"Incense?" I asked.

"Yes! I don't know what he meant by that, but it was more the way he said it to Father. It sounded the same as incest! I didn't understand his explanation—something about abusing your own family members with religion. When we catch up with him, I'll bash his skull in," she snarled, her head swinging left and right as she eyed the forest.

"Mother Abbess," snapped the priest, "be calm. Remember your blood pressure. Don't worry, we'll see that he gets what's coming to him, right, Pastor?"

"Yes, the pervert! Our poor children and the women who saw it. The Bible says very clearly that such shameful, disgusting...."

The Baptist minister was interrupted by a large potbellied man with a red face. "We've got laws in our village. That faker held a public meeting, and that so-called parade he organized...I assure you, he never got any permits from me or from City Hall. As mayor, I was elected by these fine, upstanding people to make sure that those kind of...of...."

"Mr. Mayor," said one of the men with a large rock in his hand, "the kids liked it, and I thought he showed you his license."

"Shut up, everyone!" shouted the priest. "This guy here doesn't know anything. We're wasting our time. Let's turn around and go back down the road to search there. Surely we can pick up his trail."

Grumbling, the mob turned around and hurried back the way they had come, Mother Abbess swinging her gold crosier like a hostile hockey player ready to maim. All the while she kept repeating, "Off with his head...Off with his head!"

The silence that followed their departure arched over me like a rainbow after a hurricane. The woods once again seemed serene and secure. No doubt about it, it was the master they were after. I began to worry for his safety. Then I heard it, so soft that at first I thought it was only a stirring of the leaves: "Nipper, Nipper."

I turned and looked behind me. About twenty feet away, from behind a large tree trunk, I could see what appeared to be a wisp of white beard sticking out. Two or three feet lower down the tree trunk, a finger emerged and beckoned me. I stood up and walked toward the tree. On the other side, leaning against the tree, eating a carrot, was the Master! My eyebrows arched when I saw the trickle of blood on his forehead.

"It's nothing, Nipper, a rock just grazed me. It's just a scratch. Now there's an audience that was really moved by my talk. Friend, that's what I call a good response."

"Good, Master? They were so angry they wanted to kill you! What did you say or do that made them so angry? Especially Mother Abbess—she and that priest were so upset about your 'incense,' accusation. What else did you say or do? And what was that about showing the mayor your license—what license?"

"Nipper, hold your horses—or rather my horse," he replied, handing me his hobbyhorse. "I could answer one question at a time, or I could give you a shotgun answer that would cover all the questions at once.... The shotgun answer is: I told them the truth! The truth will set you free, but it's also the truth about the marketplace, politics or religion that can get you tarred and feathered! Lest they come back this way looking for me, let's move on. I can answer your questions as we walk. It won't be safe to use the road. Let's stick to the woods and...." He paused, cocking his head to one side, and listened to the wind. "...This way. If you would hand me good old Gonnella. Let us, my noble companion, set forth with the dignity of Sir Dagonet."

"Sir who, Master?"

"Sir Dagonet! He was King Arthur's personal fool and jester. Dagonet was knighted by Arthur himself, and since these woods look like the kind that might hold the Holy Grail, let us proceed with foolish dignity."

The Master led the way, riding his hobbyhorse with such nobility that I forgot it was only a child's toy. We traveled together silently for some time, stopping now and then to listen for our pursuers. We heard only the sounds of the forest.

"They've given up the chase. Like old dogs, Nipper, they've gone back home, returned to the town to bask in the warm glow of their godly anger and righteous indignation. Let's rein-in here and rest for awhile. I'm getting too old for this kind of running around." Sitting down, he leaned back against a large oak tree. "Now to the questions you asked earlier.

"The License I showed the mayor? I've got one. See!" He removed a solemn looking document from his pocket and showed it to me. It was a Fool's License! It even had an impressive gold seal at the bottom. "I'm legal in the tradition of those great fools, John Scogan, Muckle John and Dicky Pierce. In fact, until the Seventeenth Century, fools and jesters were licensed and their names recorded in court records. Even saints had jesters! St. Thomas More's jester was Patison, who was included in Holbein's painting of the famous saintly chancellor of England. Among the famous licensed fools were the likes of Triboulet, the jester of Louis XII; Thevenin de St. Leger, the French king Charles V's fool; Rahere, jester of Henry I of England and Patch, of the court of Elizabeth, wife of Henry VII.

"Patch, by the way, was another name for any fool. It was the nickname of Cardinal Wolsey's jester, Sexton. Too bad, I say, that today's cardinals in the Catholic Church, and leaders of other religious groups, don't keep a licensed jester on their staffs! But I don't want to digress: Patch as a nickname came from the patched dress worn by licensed fools. There were many other licensed jesters; I won't bore you with their names and stories. But alas, poor Muckle John, who I mentioned earlier, he was the last licensed court fool in England. Rather, poor England, Nipper, and poor world, to have become suffocated by starch and excessive seriousness."

"Your Fool's License must have expired as far as the mayor, parish priest and mother abbess were concerned. Wow, were they angry! If they had found you...."

"Nipper, if you learn your lessons," leaning over, he tapped a finger on the *HOLY FOOLS* book that lay on the ground beside me, "and pass the test, I'll see that you get your license!"

After witnessing the mob scene on the road, I wasn't sure how eager I was to become a licensed fool. No, I hadn't left home and my business to come on this adventure to become a clown, licensed or not! I was seeking to become enlightened, to be a disciple of a spiritual master. My image of enlightened beings had them seated in blissful peace with golden auras radiating out from them. This image, on the other hand, had them looking like buffoons with asses' ears and dressed in patched clothing.

"Mother Abbess, ah yes," he said as if speaking to the leaves at the top of the tree, "a case of consecrated constipation. It's a rather common ailment among full-time church folk. It seems that she and her novice mistresses came into the town square to shop and were fortunate enough to hear part of my afternoon conference. Not sure what it was, but it might have been the big sausage that ignited her pilot light."

"Sausage? I didn't know that you ate meat! Not that eating meat, or not eating meat, is a...sign of...uh...."

"Nipper, comedy and sausages go together like apple pie and cheese. At least they did at one time. Today's comedy is usually very respectable. From the earliest Greek theater, comedy has involved defusing power, and the powerful influences of life. It's taken the power of sexuality, for example, and by poking fun at it helped it find a balance in life. Rather than denying its reality in life, comedy has placed sexuality in proper proportion with the rest of life. Comics in the Roman feast of Lupercalia, celebrated near February 15, 'played around' as they did in the old Greek theater, with big sausages.

"Anyway, the early Church made eating—and playing with— sausages a sin. Today as then, She doesn't think sex is funny, no funnier than when she got the Roman emperor Constantine to outlaw sausages in the Fourth Century. Ah, but the old wiener won out. I'd guess that Mother Abbess arrived late in my talk and missed the connection of how the big Polish sausage I was using illustrated why religion can't legislate morality. Then again, she and the Baptist minister who was present may have objected to the fart."

"I'm sorry, Master, I must not have heard you correctly. You didn't say 'fart,' did you?"

"You heard correctly. Remember what you learned, Nipper. The word 'fool' comes from the Latin for 'bag of wind.' Farting once was part of the fun at feasts, that is long ago in the days of 'Merry England.' Henry II instructed that his jester should perform at dinners, '*Saltum, siffletum et pettum*, or *bumbulum*.' Translation: 'with a leap, a whistle and a fart.' A jester in *Piers Plowman*, written around 1380, complained that he'd lost his ability to 'fart in tune at feasts.' "

I shuddered to hear any more and stood up with a determined expression, saying, "I'll go and collect some dry sticks so we can have a fire. It's late. You must be tired after today. Let's spend the night here."

The master agreed with a big smile and a naughty wink. After our simple supper, he said a brief prayer to a Saint Pantaleone, whom I'd never heard of before, and was fast asleep in minutes. By the flames of the campfire, I opened my book and began to read again.

The Folly of Faith

Once **upon a time in India,** a renowned holy man had a hermitage built on the far bank of a wide, fast flowing river. Each day a milkmaid came over the river on a ferryboat and brought him some milk. Often she was very late, which annoyed the holy man. The milkmaid apologized, saying that she often had to wait for the ferryboat because it had just left or was standing on the far shore.

"Utter foolishness, all this talk about a ferryboat," cried the holy man. "Child, anyone of faith, with God's name in one's heart and on one's lips, can walk over the waters without any difficulty. A true holy person doesn't need to wait for a ferry."

The next day, the milkmaid appeared promptly, as she did on each of the following days. The holy man was delighted, but puzzled, by her promptness and asked, "How is it, child, that you are now so punctual?"

The girl replied, "Master, I am just doing as you told me. With

God's name on my lips, I now cross the river by walking on the water. My foot does not sink, nor do I have any need of the ferryboat." The holy man stood in amazement that this milkmaid, such a simple girl, had the miraculous power of walking on water. He said to her, "This is well and good, child, but I shall go myself and watch you walk upon water. Then *I* will walk with you across the river!"

Now, he was actually envious of the simple farm girl's powers and wanted to see how she did such a miraculous feat. When they came to the bank of the river, the girl's lips were silently repeating the name of God as she stepped onto the water and started across the river as lightly as a feather. The rapidly flowing water did not splash up or even touch the soles of her feet.

The holy man was amazed at her skill. Quickly gathering up the hem of his robe, he began to murmur God's name as he stepped out onto the river. While he did manage to walk on the water, he wasn't able to keep up with the milkmaid who was flying ahead of him. She turned and, seeing that he was in danger of sinking, called out, "Master, no wonder you're sinking. How is the name of God to bear you over the water when, in the very act of calling upon God, you lift up your robe for fear of getting the hem of it wet?"

Hem holding is habitual for those with only a half hearted faith. St. Peter, when invited by Jesus to walk on water, got more than his hem wet as he began to sink into the sea. St. Peter, while the first head of the Church, was more a holy falterer than a Holy Father at that moment. Jesus reprimanded him for his lack of faith: "Friend, why did you falter? What little faith you have!" (Mt. 14: 31).

Both Peter and the holy man, seeing another person do the impossible, attempted to follow. Both, however, suffered from a shortage of faith and faltered. It's not difficult to have compassionate understanding toward both men. It's not easy to step out in faith. I'm not sure that I would ever attempt to walk on water, even if I saw a great saint doing it. I wouldn't be held back so much by a fear of losing my life as of "losing face." I'm grateful that Jesus did not make water walking a condition for discipleship.

Faith, which Jesus did require of all who wished to follow him, is a quality greater than mere belief. Faith implies an unbroken attachment, a deep loyalty rising up out of a great love. It's a profound trust that overrides logical proof or material evidence. Walking on water requires a miracle of faith, since we all know by personal experience that objects heavier than water sink! If you're hungry to be something more than just a member of a church or synagogue, if you want to embrace true discipleship, you will have to increase your faith. Walking the way of discipleship requires personal behavior and choices that are impossible without unshakeable, unfaltering faith. Today more than before, living in faith is demanding.

The contemporary erosion of belief in institutions, leaders and society's "sacred cows" makes personal faith more difficult. It's easy today to lose our faith. Each age has had its share of scandals surrounding well-known religious and political figures, and ours is no different. Besides a deficit in faith in the government and society's great institutions, God also hasn't escaped our modern faith drain. Who today is willing to place a *total* trust in God? When asked to step out in faith, we hedge our bets. While believing that anything is possible with God, we fear making Peter's mistake. So, before we step out boldly in faith, we make sure that we're wearing a life preserver—or have one of several safety nets carefully strung underneath us.

Fear sucks life out of faith, and raw, old-fashioned fear abounds today in many forms. Life is crowded with fears of cancer, terrorism, losing one's job, a major recession, dying in a nursing home, catching AIDS, having to pay more for everything from gasoline to groceries, being poisoned by toxic wastes or nuclear fallout. These common fears have become permanent house guests. There is also a pack of private little fears that rent rooms in the back of our minds.

One of the most repeated Gospel admonitions is, "Do not be afraid!" In fact, it may be the great commandment for disciples of the

Way. Its frequency in Scripture is encouraging because it says that fear isn't just an affliction of our age. As a primary message of angels and of Christ, those four words are holy words. That message could be a new mantra, a mini-prayer that reconnects us to our spiritual roots. The next time you find yourself faltering or fearful, like the disciples in their little boat, as you are tossed to and fro by some storm of life, quietly repeat the prayer, "Do not be afraid." Letting those sacred words echo within you may keep you from sinking.

Although fear has always been with us, life at the dawn of a new century abounds with unique fears to test our faith. A recent news item from Holland is a great example of such tests. In Langeboom in the Netherlands, a twenty-four-year-old woman was hospitalized after doctors discovered that she had been living for four years wrapped in a plastic sheet, eating only canned food. Covered in plastic, she did not leave her living room sofa except to use the bathroom. Yet, in those four years she did not bathe once! This young woman was held prisoner in her own home by her fears over the danger of radiation from the Chernobyl, Russia nuclear power plant accident! This is a newspaper parable, a sad example of how easily fears can imprison us and force us to live cramped lives. If this news story of the woman so fearful that she lived as a prisoner in her own home wasn't so pathetic, it would be humorous! Is there a fear in your life that causes you also to live in strange, unnatural or unholy ways?

While you may not be challenged to prove your faith by walking on water, you may be called to something perhaps just as difficult. We are a future-obsessed people. Living without anxiety is not easy for those who are overly concerned about tomorrow. Corporations and institutions make their living by playing on our fears. Daily life is filled with fears that challenge our faith in a loving, caring God. Yet, our faith isn't proven by embracing Church dogmas but by struggling to live with hope and without fear. If your faith gauge shows that you have only a little, don't be too concerned. A little faith is enough! Recall how Jesus said that even if our faith was as little as a mustard seed, it could move mountains! Peter and the other first disciples started with only a little faith, but they were able to cause it to grow large enough to be the source of countless miracles and miraculous deeds of courage. Fear not, then, if your faith is small—for it can grow.

Interested in increasing your faith? Friend, I have just what you need! For only $4.99, we will mail directly to your home a box of MIRACLE-GROW. You no longer need to be ashamed if you have just a little dab of faith. Just water it daily with MIRACLE-GROW, and you will be amazed at the results. In a matter of weeks, friend, you too can have your own miracles.

Why spend money on pilgrimages to far-off shrines or expensive visits to faith healers and gurus? Now you and your friends can enjoy miracles in the privacy of your own home or back yard. Don't delay, why suffer from a puny faith? Send today for this Faith Fertilizer. Cash or major credit cards taken. NO personal checks, however—my faith in human nature is limited.

Faith Fertilizer? Well, I admit that a teaspoon of MIRACLE-GROW in a glass of water daily may not give you the ability to walk on water—the FDA requires making that disclaimer. However, in the humor is hidden the truth that faith can be fertilized. Plant foods can do wonders for vegetables and flowers, and faith is like flowers—all it needs is a little fertilizer. What fertilizes faith is using it. The results of regular exercise may not be spectacular, like walking on water, but you will experience God's daily providential love and care. Each time you step out in faith and trust God, you create the fertile possibility of a personalized faith experience.

A recent Gallup Poll asked Americans the source of their faith. The poll revealed some interesting facts. Only 3% said that their source was religious authorities and leaders! 31% reported that the Bible, Torah or Koran was the source of their faith. The majority, however, over 46%, said it was—a la St. Thomas—personal experience! Since personal experience is our most common source of faith, a wise disciple would do well to seize every opportunity to personally know God's providential care. If you desire to deepen your faith, one of the best ways to begin is by being willing to take more risks!

First, challenge yourself to get out from underneath your plastic sheet and leave the sofa of your security systems. Don't be like that poor woman in Holland. Faith grows each time it's proven valid. Give God a chance to prove to you how much you are loved. For that to happen requires a real willingness to take risks in life. That further requires becoming a lover, since risking is easier for lovers. Faith is the flower of love. The greater your love for someone, the greater your confidence in that person. As you daily grow in your love of God by prayer and devotion, you will discover that your faith is also growing—as is your willingness to leave your security sofa and begin to take chances.

Second, cultivate long-standing friendships and love relationships. People of faith generally have faithful friendships that span the years and are personal proofs of fidelity, loyalty and commitment. Since God is love, each loving friendship that has proven dependable increases your faith in God's abiding care. Jesus' intimate union with the Divine Mystery, a relationship of great love and affection, was the source of his profound sense of trust in God's providential care. That pattern of loving relationship is available to us all.

Third, celebrate anniversaries and "Do you remember when" occasions. Such times reinforce our faith because they are personal history events of fidelity. Sacred rituals that remember past divine deeds shared with family or friends of the same faith are fruitful for personal fidelity and provide symbolic models for taking risks. These sacred rituals are Umbrella Faith Celebrations intended to be broad enough to include a remembrance of all the personal experiences that have validated our faith. Faith grows in the act of remembering. Religious-remembrance rituals are truly important, especially when we secretly insert into them our personal faith stories.

Fourth, develop a life-vision that is creative and vital. Our faith is shaped by what we expect from life. A positive, hope-filled vision of life not only needs a faith in God but also in ourselves. Part of such a faith vision is the fertile belief that with God's help we can transform misfortune into a blessing. A Portuguese proverb says, "God writes straight with crooked lines." In 1914 Thomas Edison's laboratories burned down, causing the loss of over two million dollars worth of equipment and the records of many years of experiments. Edison was sixty-seven years old, and in the morning as he stood in the midst of the ruins of his laboratories he said to his son, "Charles, there is great value in disaster. All our mistakes are burned up! Thank God we can start anew." Such an attitude is the fruit of years of personal experiments in seeing every misfortune as an easily "missed" fortune.

The next time you're on the verge of faltering in your faith when you're faced with a crisis or a full-blown disaster, don't run away! Instead, see the crisis as a gift-opportunity to grow in faith. Regardless of how small your faith may seem to you, remember that even a little faith goes a long way. Use what little you have and as you do you will discover an amazing secret: the more you use the little you have, the greater it will grow!

Exercises:

DON'T BE AFRAID TO PICKAX YOUR FAITH

Questioning matters of faith is sometimes judged as wrong or even sinful. Faith, however, is a belief in that which is unseen and so is always pregnant with questions. To question deep realities you need to go well beneath the surface. Such exploration leads to enlightenment and is a healthy part of growing in faith. Be alert and ask the right questions. In examining events in Scripture, rather than asking, "Did it happen?" try, "What does it mean?" Such questions, if sharp and used with great love, are as useful as pickaxes in a gold mine.

PREVENT FAITH LEAKAGE AND A DULL SOUL

When you're overworked and tired, it's difficult to be faithful. It's easy to become angry and view life negatively when you are under stress. Albert Schweitzer said that some people "simply let their souls wither. They allow themselves to be dulled by the...worries and distractions of life...."

To prevent a withered, dull soul—and one parched of faith—be good to yourself and frequently retreat to rest. Take a day off to relax on a regular basis. The older you are, the more you need extended time off to renew yourself both in body and soul—two or three days in a row.

The reward? You'll renew your faith in God and in the basic goodness of life.

FAITH IS CONTAGIOUS

Associate with the Hopeful

Since faith is an attitude of life, it is influenced by all of your life—especially those closest to you. Associate with those who are positive in thinking and speech. Their optimistic outlook will nourish your growing faith. Listen with respect to others' stories of minor miracles. Value them as private gospels from which you can learn to trust more deeply. Be cautious of the company of cynics and those who always find something wrong. After visiting with such people always wash your hands—and your mind.

Clowning with Conflicts

A **renowned** **contemporary classic clown** was Charlie Chaplin whose old silent films had him prophetically playing with the problem of machines. His comedy routine of being caught up in the wheels of giant monster machines, like the warnings of Old Testament prophets, spoke of an impending disaster in which technology snags people in its mechanical talons. Such jester-clowns as Chaplin force us to confront our problems and the predicament of our world.

As once the nobility assembled at the king's court and peasants gathered in front of the steps of great medieval cathedrals to be amused, contemporary comics have the power to help us laugh and play with the problems of our day. For fool-jesters, problems become toys, a source of entertainment and inner-attainment.

One ninety-year-old man was suffering from a minor affliction and went to the doctor. He hadn't been to a physician in twenty-five years, so he was asked to fill out a medical history. After the usual questions about various diseases and ailments, the doctor, who practiced holistic medicine, asked, "Tell me, how was your childhood?"

The old man thought for a moment and answered, "Well, Doc, so far, so good!"

At ninety years of age, would that you and I could make the same response. Regardless of our age, we should never outgrow childhood. Remaining ever youthful, however, isn't easy since worries age us so rapidly. Anxieties and cares wrinkle our skin and rob us of childhood. Perhaps the greatest thieves of peace and childhood are the problems which cause our anxieties.

One test to see if we are still in our childhood comes in the question, "Do you still enjoy toys and playing?" Recently I saw a toy designed for children ages one and one-half to five. It was composed of two parts: a plastic box with a dozen or more holes of different shapes and a collection of plastic pieces that fit the holes. The toy presents a child with the problem of finding the properly shaped piece to fit each hole. That very process of going from hole to hole is pure play to a child. After many unsuccessful attempts, the piece fits perfectly into its appropriate hole, and the result is the joy of discovery—that is, if you're a child.

Adults are conditioned to become frustrated, upset and angry when the piece they are attempting to put into a hole doesn't fit. They usually try to force the piece into the hole directly in front of them instead of going playfully in search of an opening that fits the piece at hand. If the adults in question are "religious," they might not become angry but would likely turn to prayer instead: "Oh, God, change the shape of the hole to fit the piece I'm trying to force into it." If you took a poll of your own prayers, would not most of them be about life's various problems: a difficulty with a child, a marriage problem, a financial problem or even the problem of how to pray? At the core of our problem-prayers is asking God for a miracle, asking God to change the shape of the hole! Unlike a small child, we do not often find delight in problem solving. Most adults attempt to avoid problems by denying their existence—until it's impossible not to deal with them.

Today's popular expression, "Have a good day," implies a day free of problems, devoid of difficulties. A good day is a "peaceful" one, without interpersonal conflicts, the weather ideal—a day in which everything "works." Jesus promised us the gift of peace, but he said, "I give you peace, yet not as the world gives peace" (Jn. 14: 27). The peace of the world is a "good day." The peace of Christ, however, can exist no matter how rocky or unpleasant our day might be. Even if a day is bad according to the world's gauge, it can be peaceful because one's problems are viewed differently.

A day undisturbed by problems isn't a "good day" for a child: it's a dull day. It's colorless because it has no play. Are not most childhood toys problem solving toys? Games like jig-saw puzzles epitomize our primal playful search for the right pieces which we fit together to form a picture. Life is like a jig-saw puzzle or a toy box with countless different difficulties. There are many problem pieces that don't seem to fit, pieces we usually try to force into the wrong holes. Yet life's problems, like children's toys, are intended to be educational.

Put down this book, take a few minutes and name some problem in your life at this moment. Whatever the problem, it can be educational because it's fertile with the potential for new growth—if you approach it with a different attitude. In the play of problems, you must first probe the possibility that what needs to change isn't the shape of the hole but something in you. The usual adult approach to a problem is that something in the other person or in the external conditions must change. Interpersonal problems challenge us to reexamine our way of thinking. We are forced to look at our expectations about how life is *supposed* to be.

In Greek the source of our word "problem" implies playfulness,

since it literally means "something thrown forward." A problem is like a ball or Frisbee tossed in the air that we are invited to playfully chase. It suggests the playfulness of animals, like dogs who delight in chasing after objects. Animals play for the same reason as children: to enjoy life and to learn. Why should adulthood signal an end to the play of learning? If we wish to remain youthful, regardless of our age, we should examine our prayers. When a problem appears, instead of praying that it be removed, we can ask of God, "What attitudes, expectations or ways of thinking do I need to change?" Don't expect to hear an immediate reply, however, since when God tells us that something inside must change, that message usually encounters a closed and locked door. Patience is required until the door of the heart opens to personal change and transformation.

Life's play of problems also requires the patient pursuit of the properly shaped slot for a particular problem. Patience is productive waiting. So while we search for the right slot, we can take out our gift of imagination and do something productive.

If our imagination is asleep, we need to wake it up, since play requires a use of active imagination. As small children, this God-given talent was wide-awake and allowed us to see life from novel perspectives. As we grew up, however, that birth-gift was slowly anesthetized. We went to school where we learned very quickly that knowledge is

more important than imagination. Growing up with a television for a nanny, unlike playing with a radio or storytelling, required no use of the imagination. Then, when we entered the work force, we discovered that the "powers that be" in the business world and the Church were not only uninterested in innovation, they feared it. Yet even in the face of all these oppressive factors, we have cause not to abandon hope. Our imaginations aren't dead, but only asleep!

Daily we can practice imaging new ways to resolve our problems. The more we play with it, the more the imagination will awaken and become an ally. We are called to regard all our problems with the awareness that all things work for the good for those who love God. Problems can be approached with an attitude that hidden inside of them are gifts of newness, seeds of something better than what existed before. Mindful of the power of words, we can rename our difficulties. Rather than calling them problems, which has a negative connotation, we can call them mysteries, games or spiritual exercises. Louis Kahn exercised this kind of creative renaming by describing streets as "rivers" and parking lots as "harbors." Such new names hold the magical power to change old attitudes about driving. The same can be true for any of the difficulties in life's playpen of problems.

Jesus is the prototype of problem resolvers. While he had more than his share of problems, he didn't lose his peace, his harmony with God.

The Gospels are full of stories of how Jesus dealt with dilemmas. His enemies in the orthodox right were constantly proposing religious problems in an attempt to trap him. To each of their deadly "Gotcha" games, he replied with imagination and creativity. His inspired answers flowed from an ability to view any issue from a new angle. This ability to see a crisis in a new way is especially evident in one story when his disciples came to him with a big problem. They were anxious because there wasn't enough food to feed the crowd of thousands who had followed him out into the wasteland. His reply to their problem turned it into an educational experience. He said, "You feed them! Break and share the bread, you have with those seated nearby. By sharing your bread you'll start a wave of sharing that will sweep across this vast hungry crowd" (See Mt. 14: 14-21).

Jesus ultimately took the world's oldest problem, the grim reality of aging and death and, with the Holy Spirit as a playmate, created something new in his resurrection. He resolved the problem of death by showing that it is not the end but only a stage of life. If you believe that, you will be free of the fear of dying. That freedom can open the floodgates of creativity. Otto Rank, the famous psychologist, said that an artist's greatest obstacle to creativity is the fear of death. Today, when so many once stable institutions are dying, is our inability to respond to that reality in a creative way due to our lack of faith? Do we truly believe that death, any death, is part of life?

Jesus also took the world's second oldest problem, selfishness, and gave us an innovative solution. The problem is that our personal needs always insist on being at the head of the line: my own needs come before the needs of others.  Selfishness is the source of most of the problems in our personal lives—

and most of the world's problems. Jesus' invitation to his followers at the Last Supper was his antidote to the problem. He invited us "to remember," to repeat again and again the giving away of ourselves, body and blood, in daily life as well as in ritual. "Do this..." and you will create a new way of thinking. Richard Pascale in his book, *Managing on the Edge: How the Smartest Companies Use Conflict to Stay Ahead,* said that creativity is born of tension, passion and conflict. It is easier to act ourselves into a better mode of thinking than to think ourselves into a better mode of acting. Reflect on that thought, mindful of how you and I, and the rest of the world, are attempting to "manage on the edge." We are on the edge of an emerging new world as the old one falls away. Teetering on the edge, let us pray for the passion necessary to act creatively and unselfishly. Since tension and conflict abound on the edge, what is needed most is passionate love.

One practical exercise to deal with the problem of selfishness would be to perform three acts of unselfishness each day with as much passion as possible. At the end of a day, we can check to see if all three were performed. Those left undone would be added to the next day. Doing this daily for a month will develop a habit. With the passage of time, this habit of acting unselfishly will evolve into a habitude. A habitude is more than an attitude, it's an almost unconsciously "natural" behavior that for the disciple of Jesus is really supernatural. A Christlike spirituality is nothing more than developing the habitude of Jesus. It is a lifestyle of giving away ourselves, of denying our self with passion, with love. It is this habitude of Christ which makes possible responding to problems without the loss of peace and balance.

An important part of the habitude of Jesus is his fondness for prayer. Whether or not he retreated to some mountain, his prayer always elevated him. Whenever I think of him praying on a mountain top, I imagine him seated at its peak, looking down on his village with all its problems. From that vantage point, his village must have appeared rather small, and its problems even smaller. Prayer gives us a new attitude because it provides the proper altitude. Our daily problems need to be put in proportion if we are to respond to them without anxiety or anger. The next time some big problem pounces on you, remember to pray. Using the great gift of your imagination, climb a great mountain and look at your life. From that elevation see your new problem in its proper proportion, its true relationship to the most important things in your life.

The poor of his day came to Jesus with problems concerning clothing, food and money, with anxieties about what might happen tomorrow. From his habitude of elevated

It often takes two "children" to make a "big" problem manageable.

prayer, Jesus urged them not to be anxious about such minor issues. He told them to be concerned instead with what is really important in life: Life itself. He spoke with conviction because by prayer he had himself placed the problems of *his* life in their proper proportion.

Over the centuries the same old problems have robbed people of happiness and peace. The problems that the crowds brought to Jesus 2,000 years ago are the same problems we face, only their clothes are new. We can teach ourselves to respond to problems with playfulness, creatively renaming them and viewing them as educational toys. If we learn to look at them from every possible angle, especially from a high altitude, we may find to our delight that they are not burdens but blessings.

Exercises:

PROBLEM SOLVING REQUIRES ASKING THE RIGHT QUESTION

Years ago the city of Los Angeles had the problem of how to move the growing number of cars through the city. Failing to ask the right question, they built a massive freeway system to solve their problem of rapid transportation. The result is that the average speed today on their freeways during rush hour is about the rate of a horse and carriage! The correct question might have been, "How do we move large numbers of people from one place to another in our city?" By constructing more highways they only increased the problem.

Take time to make sure that you are asking the correct question about whatever problem you are facing.

THE OIL CAKE PROBLEM:
AN EXAMPLE OF HOW PROBLEMS HIDE THE PROMISE OF HIDDEN TREASURES AND NEW BEGINNINGS

Over two hundred years ago the Dutch created the *olykoek*, or oil cake. This small, round sweetened dough-cake, sometimes covered with sugar, was cooked by dropping it in hot oil. There was, however, a problem of uniform frying. Often cakes would come out with a soggy center. Legend says that in 1847 Hanson Gregory solved the problem by poking holes in the center of the little oil cakes, increasing the surface area for uniform frying. The next time you eat a doughnut, rejoice in Gregory's resolution to a problem.

Try poking holes in your problems and you might come up with a new creation that will delight not only you but the whole world. On an average day, Dunkin' Donuts alone serves 2,739,726 of Hanson Gregory's creative solutions.

A PRAYERFUL WAY TO PLAY WITH PROBLEMS

1. Acknowledge to yourself that there is a problem! Be aware of how it makes you angry and upset. Often we are upset because we feel out of control and trapped by a problem. Let go of the illusion of being in control of life: it's a fantasy. Embrace reality and let God embrace you.

2. Play with the problem by turning it over and over as you would with a new, unknown toy. Use your imagination to explore different ways to resolve it. Let such exploration have no limits. Dance with it, laugh about it, sing a song about it. Let your humorous play entertain even bizarre solutions.

3. Next, ask yourself if this problem hides something you really enjoy, something that you need to do but haven't had time for. Take an elevator to the top floor and look back down at your problem to see how important it is in relation to the rest of your life.

4. View your problem as a spiritual exercise, the purpose of which is to help you grow into a more godlike person. Be aware that your problem may have global consequences, calling forth heroic behavior, as it did with such "situational saints" as Francis of Assisi, Joan of Arc and Gandhi.

The Story Gets Lonely

My eyes were full of sleep. The last few sentences I read were fused together in fuzziness. It was time for me to seek the embrace of Morpheus, the god of sleep and dreams. Crawling inside my bedroll, I quickly fell asleep.

I was awakened by someone tapping on wood. I opened my eyes, surprised to see that the sun had been up for hours! Having overslept for so long made me feel like Epimenides, the ancient poet and religious teacher of Crete. Epimenides is said to have fallen asleep in a cave as a boy, only to awaken fifty-seven years later. He was an ancient Greek Rip Van Winkle. However, when Epimenides awoke, he discovered that he possessed all wisdom. Although I felt as rested as if I had slept for years, unlike Epimenides, I didn't feel any wiser than the night before.

Looking about, I saw what had awakened me. It was a woodpecker busy getting its breakfast from a nearby tree. I also saw that the Master was gone. His bedroll was neatly folded up. On top of the bedroll was a note.

Dear Nipper,

Good morning! I trust you had a good night's rest. Be an obedient disciple, and don't come after me. I awoke, remembering that an old friend has his hermitage in this forest. It's a few miles from here. I've gone to visit him and will return shortly.

I left you a gift, a souvenir: my old straight razor. While I haven't used it in years, you can use it as a centering image for meditation. May its narrow sharp edge remind you that the Way's as narrow as a razor's edge. Till I return, reflect on it, study your book, practice patience and your exercises and...the art of farting!

Love,

Window Sill

Since I had no idea which way he had gone, it was easy to be an obedient disciple. After a simple breakfast, I opened my Hobbyhorse Handbook. As the warmth of the sun filtered through the trees, I realized the unique experience of spending so much time in nature. I didn't realize that my experience would be directly addressed in the chapter I was about to read.

Spirituality for under the Big Top

ircus tents were the big tops under which lived a wondrous world of entertainment for both adult and child. It amazed and dazzled, surprised and delighted one and all. Such is the Big Top of the great blue dome of the sky which arches over the earth. Few, however, are eager to enter this Big Top.

Harper's Index recently reported this amazing fact: "Americans spend only 2% of their lives out-of-doors!" Consider the implications of the fact that we spend 98% of our lives inside our homes, work places or vehicles. We can wonder too how much of that tiny percentage of time in nature is spent walking on concrete or asphalt. When you further consider the fact that the "average" includes farmers, fishermen, construction workers and others who work mostly out-of-doors, the actual amount of living most people do outside shrinks to minute proportions. This study helps us realize how divorced we are from earth and creation at the dawning of a new millennium.

A good religion and a healthy spirituality should lead us to wholeness and holiness. The prophet Isaiah, on experiencing his awesome mystical vision of God in the Temple of Jerusalem, cried out, "Holy, Holy, Holy are you, O God. Heaven and earth are full of your glory." If the earth is indeed filled with the glory of God, with the divine presence, shouldn't an experience of the earth be an important part of our prayer? Has our experience of God become an indoor reality; can God only be worshiped indoors?

How can we truly be whole persons if we spend 98% of our lives separated from the divine glory and the healing powers in the earth, sea and air? Today, Christianity is certainly an indoor religion. While it proclaims the glory of God in creation and frequently makes references to nature in its official prayers and hymns, as a religion it seems very uncomfortable unless it is under a roof and contained within four walls. Furthermore, today we prefer, if not demand, that our sacred space be air-conditioned and have central heating. Occasionally, there is an exception, like a Palm Sunday procession or an Easter Sunday sunrise service held outside. The only religious service, however, that is consistently performed outside is the burial rite. Even at the cemetery we often prefer that tents be erected, with appropriate fake green turf spread over the recently dug-up earth so that we don't have to be exposed to the bare dirt. Other than a few references to the earth of the grave, the ritual prayers of these burial services seldom acknowledge that one is in the midst of creation.

One of the activities that's part of the 2% of our lives spent outdoors is eating. A meal shared in nature has its own name: a picnic. A real picnic has its own rituals and special equipment, and a real picnic implies finger food and sharing it while seated directly on the earth! Unfortunately, we often try to make even the precious moments of these outdoor family rituals as much like indoors as possible. Picnic tables, on patios and in back yards, are common middle-upper-class pieces of furniture. Any self-respecting park provides picnic tables, often on cement, for those who want to dine out-of-doors. Yet this furnishing is a rather recent concession to our discomfort at being outside. If you

look at old paintings or photographs of picnics, you will see people seated on blankets placed directly on the earth. But that, of course, is where the ants and other bugs live! It seems we are more comfortable the more we are able to keep nature at a safe distance. However, there is a price we pay for separating ourselves from nature so that we can be comfortable. In keeping a safe distance from discomfort, we also unfortunately block ourselves from the restorative powers of nature and from the awesome power of the divine.

If we are honest, we have to admit that contemporary Jewish, Islamic and Christian spiritualities are all anti-creation. That fact is especially remarkable for Christians, since all of the great events in the life of Christ which we commemorate and celebrate, except for his Last Supper, occurred in the midst of nature! How seemingly strange is our custom of celebrating those historically holy outdoor events indoors. Perhaps the avoidance of nature has arisen from how Christianity grew up in the cities of the Near East, Greece and Italy. Our urban bias is reflected in the term for those who are non-believers. The word "pagan" comes from the Latin *paganus* which means "country-dweller." Those in the country were the last to give up their nature gods and their religions that centered around the awesome mysteries of nature. The reaction of the early Church to these natural religions is understandable. But do we still need to fear that if we go outside to pray or worship we will return to worshiping trees and rivers?

If we wish to develop a wholesome spirituality, we will have to go out-of-doors a good deal more often than 2% of our lifetimes. Creation holds great powers to heal us, to soothe over the cares and stresses of our daily lives. We need to do more than look at nature from our windows, or even from our screened-in porches. We need to return to that environment which is our primal home, to the milieu with which we were created to live in harmony. Within the human heart is a hunger to do precisely that. This longing to be in touch with creation can even be recognized on entering many large buildings or shopping malls. Architects, sensitive to the hungers of our hearts, have created vast glass domes overhead so we can see the clouds and sky. They have created spaces for trees, fountains and flower gardens to help us feel at home. But these carefully controlled, artificial indoor environments are still a full step away from a direct contact with nature.

Perhaps, too, you are one of the many who have potted plants in your home, office or church. Such a desire to bring the outdoors inside is an expression of that same hunger to be one with nature. Again, however, it's on *our* terms. According to recent figures released by the National Pest Control Association, Americans spend a record $3,500,000,000 (that's 3½ billion!) each year trying to eradicate household pests. We want nature inside, true, but only some of it. In a humorous aside to this report, when Pittsburgh residents were asked which household pests they feared most, 1.3% responded by naming family members!

Each delightful season of the year, full of its own unexpected surprises like snowstorms and rain showers, sings a siren's song, calling us out-of-doors from our comfortable, climate-controlled cocoons. Spring, for example, breathes her seductive perfumes through the cracks of our houses and awakens primal urges to plant seeds in the ground or go out for a walk. Summer calls us to leisurely afternoons at the beach or evenings at the park. Autumn invites us to take in an awesome color show and winter to breathtaking snowscapes and exquisite stillness. Even in areas where there is little or no change of season or dramatic scenery, nature is full of subtle yet remarkable wonders.

A good way to begin to create a wholesome spirituality is to give in to the seasons' siren songs and risk letting nature embrace you with her healing gifts. Naturally, it's easier to be in communion with creation if you are a pagan, that is, a *paganus*, a country-dweller. Yet, while it's more difficult if you live in an apartment in some crowded city, it's also more important that you give in to creation's temptation. You will find that it's worth every bit of time and effort to seek out a park or spend some time in the country.

We can also learn from the Japanese. For centuries they have lived crowded together on a tiny island no larger than the state of Montana with a population half the size of the United States. Traditionally, each family has built a rock garden behind its small home. It was a miniature version of the wilderness with a small pool of water to reflect the sea and a large rock to represent a mountain. They would go to their tiny gardens to be refreshed and re-created by creation.

If you are fortunate enough to have a little lawn around your home, consider spending some time in the most ancient of all professions: caring for it yourself. Adam and Eve were the first gardeners; it was in fact their primary vocation. I don't know if they had to mow the lawn or even if in that Eden paradise there were any weeds. Our need, however, to keep what little nature surrounds our homes looking beautiful is but an extension of the work of our first parents. I realize that you, like the rest of us, are very busy with many matters of consequence. Perhaps some of you even can afford to hire one of the numerous lawn-care companies or some kid down the block to do those time consuming tasks for you. However, you might consider your yard maintenance as an invitation to enter into and enjoy being one with nature. Some of you may be so seduced as to plant and care for a garden of flowers or vegetables. It could be the "Adam's apple" a day that keeps the doctor away.

Sharing your life with tame animals, birds, reptiles or fish is another natural spiritual exercise that can prove to be very prayerful because it brings you into communion with a primal part of who you are, as well as part of the real world. Yet another spiritual practice is to go for a walk, regardless of the weather. In fact, you might be surprised by the sacred, sensual pleasure of taking a walk in the rain. Of course, you will get wet! You may return home looking like a rat that just swam ashore, but a lot of daily grit and grime will have been washed away from your soul. And I promise that you will feel more human for having done so.

When we were kids, we always wanted to go outside when it was raining or snowing. Our parents wouldn't let us for fear we would catch cold—or ruin our clothes. Now that we are adults, however, and in control of our own lives, we rarely want to go outside anymore. When we live inside, each hair on our heads stays in place. We are not bothered by bugs and flies and we keep comfortable with just the right temperature level. By not wanting to disturb our comfort zones, often without realizing it, our habitats have become habitual.

Today we hear a great deal about space stations that someday will be orbiting planet Earth. The very thought of being in a space colony and living totally inside an artificial environment, without benefit of open windows and fresh air, without the pleasure of feeling upon one's skin the changing of the seasons or having one's hands in the rich soil of the earth, can give one a feeling of claustrophobia. Yet if the Harper Index is correct, you and I are only 2% away from being ideal candidates for such a life in space!

Exercise-Diagram:

MOUNTAIN "STANDING STONE"

MOUND FOR STONE — DIRT REMOVED FROM POOL HOLE

FLAT STONES TO HIDE TUB TOP

LOW EVER-GREENS

POOL

OLD WASH TUB OR STOCK TANK BURIED

ROCKS FOR SMALL HILLS

DO-IT-YOURSELF MINI-ZEN-GARDEN~

Fools Rush into Prison

"**F**ools rush in** where angels fear to tread," and only a fool would rush into prison where, in contemporary society, conditions are so terrible that even angels would have a hard time. Only a fool would want to "do time" in overcrowded, often inhumane jails or prisons. Imagine the shock of unbelieving guards if someone came knocking at their prison gate, begging to be admitted!

Holy Fool, find yourself a closet prison cell and joyfully lock yourself up! Madness—since anyone who feels that prison might even be a possibility would likely hire the best lawyer that funds allow, would plea bargain or perhaps even seek asylum in a church or embassy to prevent being imprisoned. The overcrowded conditions and destructive environment of our jails make this understandable, but prison, paradoxically, is a place to which each one of us frequently should go.

The idea of "doing time" in enforced solitude is near the bottom of just about everyone's list of fun and desirable activities. Yet enforced solitude is *the* source of sanctity and creativity. If you are seeking the holiness held up in the Gospels and the great religious traditions, if you seek the ultimate human realization, then Prison Prayer should be an essential part of your

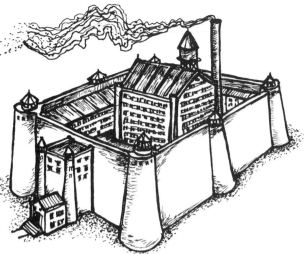

life. To help you appreciate this strange sounding advice a little prison history might be valuable.

Our present prison system is an American invention of the last decades of the Eighteenth Century. Today's inhumane system of imprisonment for those judged guilty of violating the law is certainly more a form of punishment than reform. While the prison system itself is in need of radical reform, it can be a good metaphor for exploring the seemingly crazy behavior of solitary confinement found in the lives of prophets and saints.

Our "penitentiary" concept and the name for prisons originated with the Quakers of Philadelphia. Quakers desired a more humane substitute for the death penalty and the brutal corporal punishment that was prevalent at the time. Long interested in correcting the terrible conditions which existed in English and American prisons, the Quakers advocated total silence and the penitential aspects of isolation as a way to reform criminals. The penitentiary was to be a place of prolonged silent retreat which would lead the prisoner to a reform of heart.

The first penitentiaries were operated under the "separate and silent system." Each prisoner spent the entire length of his sentence in solitary confinement in a tiny 3' x 7' x 7' cell. Because some prisoners went insane or died, the Auburn system was introduced, whereby inmates would work and eat together but return to their private cells each night. This "congregate and silent system" forbade the prisoner from speaking to anyone at anytime. Until the 1930's many of our prisons required that prisoners maintain silence at all times.

Such a prison "retreat," with enforced solitude and silence, designed to enable the prisoner reflecting on his criminal behavior to turn his life around, might have been ideal for the Quakers. It was not, however, as we well know, a successful solution to the question of how to deal with the criminals of society. However, while the penitentiary system has not often led to the reformation of contemporary criminals, it can provide a model for those who wish to both reform their hearts and to grow spiritually.

The heart of the model lies in the *enforced* solitude and silence. Not so long ago, going on retreat was seen as an important ingredient for those seeking more than a Sunday-to-Sunday relationship with God. Retreat time was really prison time, concentrated silence and solitude, spent either separately or with others. In the past twenty years, however, the classic retreat has largely been replaced by a variety of models, such as group discussions, encounters, shared prayer and even sports events—all with little, if any, silence. Just as modern pilgrimages have turned pilgrims into little more than religious tourists, so retreats for many are no more than spiritual holidays from work and family responsibilities. For those who seriously seek a reform of heart, perhaps it's time to return to the sobering solitude and silence of those early Quaker model prisons!

Prison Prayer is the opposite of spontaneous prayer since it implies *enforced* solitude. The need for privacy and personal solitude is present in everyone's life. Yet this need for solitude is one which we seek to control because when it becomes uncomfortable, when the walls begin closing in, the natural response is to want to quickly get out. Prison Prayer locks us in; during the time of prayer we are not free to come and go as we desire. This could be for a period of days, as in the classic retreat, or a matter of hours or even minutes, as when we predetermine how long we will spend in meditation or prayer.

Since solitary confinement seems so unproductive, those who still go on retreat tend to bring suitcases filled with books to read, tapes to listen to and projects to accomplish. Even old-fashioned retreats had frequent conferences in which a retreat director provided input for reflection. But the power of solitary confinement resides in the absence of activity, even pious reading intended to feed the spirit. Being imprisoned with oneself bears fruit because there is no escape from reflective thinking. We all naturally resist such a house of mirrors since what we are forced to see can be so threatening. It is only natural to fear that in such a serious examination of our personal commitments, our way of life and our daily work, we might choose to do something else. So we plod on, keeping ourselves busy and constantly committed so that we don't have to face such an unpleasant possibility. And even those who do pray daily or take time for retreats tend to keep these times as full as possible, lest the "truth" might visit them.

The value of silence and solitude in our lives has been overshadowed by a compulsive need to talk and to share. If you have a problem today, the customary solution is to "talk it out" with someone. And so

we have as wide a range of experts to talk with as we have problems. While therapy and support groups have real worth, solitude offers us an irreplaceable way to discover, evaluate and "own" a problem. Voluntary solitary confinement is unique in its capacity to help us find the root of an issue. When we truly face into our own predicaments, as deeply as we can, we find a grace that leads to freedom.

However, enforced solitude seems to be a punishment worse than death since we are, by nature, communal beings. As children we knew the punishment of being sent to our room and having to sit there in silence. As adults we have all tasted the excommunication of the old "silent treatment," when someone we had offended sentenced us to the painful prison of rejection. And so it is understandable that we might want to reject solitude as being in any way a valuable experience. Who would voluntarily choose solitary confinement?

To mention only a few: Moses took a forty day retreat on Mt. Sinai; Buddha sat still for seven years under the Bo Tree; Jesus went into the desert for forty days, as well as making frequent retreats to remote places; and the Prophet Mohammed went off on his solitary desert retreats. Each of these spiritual trailblazers freely chose the penitential values of enforced solitude. They took along no books or other distractions that might prevent them from the work of their prison prayer. The lives of the saints are full of stories about the enforced solitude imposed on them by recovery from sickness, leading to the

reformation of their lives. Solitude, freely chosen, imposed by sickness or even while in prison itself, has also produced some of the great works of literature. Reflecting on this, why not choose it for yourself?

If you are serious about heeding the core message of Jesus to "Reform your heart, for the Kingdom of God is at hand" (Mt. 3: 2), you might want to consider imitating his voluntary solitary confinement. You could sentence yourself to prison, to the isolation and the silence of a retreat at home or away. It is even possible to pass this sentence not so much as a punishment but as a pleasurable experience. Saint Paul proudly called himself "a prisoner of the Lord" when he wrote from his prison cell. You might take that title for yourself when you freely choose a reformatory experience. The old Country song, "I'm Just a Prisoner of Love," suggests the real motivation for entering into such a lonely desert experience. Love alone is the reason for any reform of heart: love of God, love of self, a love of life and the world that will be different when your heart is reformed. It is impossible to love life fully and deeply without finding the ground that solitude opens to us.

Here are a few turn-of-the-century models for prison-style retreats. Once a year it can be valuable to go on a full retreat, withdrawing yourself from daily life. Retreat to some place designed to provide the necessary solitude. This could be a house of prayer, a monastery or retreat center or even a vacation cabin at the lake. However, go on this retreat with as little in your suitcase as possible. A solitary environment can really breed creativity. But once a year, at least, take along no books, audio tapes or projects to accomplish. If you must have a book, let it be God's Book, and read little but reflect a lot. Jesus, I'm sure, took no book or scroll with him into the desert! We've all heard enough conferences or sermons about what we should do. We all mostly need time to reflect on what we have done with what we have heard and read. When you go on retreat, bring along only a desire to sit in the mirror-house of Quaker prison solitude and to have your heart reformed in the process.

You can also make a do-it-yourself retreat in your own home, setting aside an hour or a morning or an afternoon. Select a place as bare, as cell-like, as possible so you won't be distracted by familiar objects or by the "white" noise of things that shout out commands like, "Dust me" or "Put me in order." You could choose a corner in the basement, sit in your car or—and this may sound strange—an empty closet! What is important is that it be a place which can lend itself to your going inward for reflection.

Shorter daily periods of silent sitting, of meditation, are retreat times which offer valuable space for an ongoing reform of heart. It is important to "sentence" yourself to a specific period of time so that you are not free to escape from the solitude when it becomes disturbing. Your prison sentence might be ten, twenty or thirty minutes, but give yourself no parole from the time you have set aside.

Besides those daily times of prayer withdrawal, it can be very valuable to sentence yourself to solitary confinement whenever you find yourself in conflict with others. Sitting still and doing nothing when angry or upset can be most painful, but it can also be extremely productive. This form of prison prayer provides an opportunity to be both parent and child when we realize we have been naughty. We can send ourselves to our bedroom, voluntarily isolating ourselves for the purpose of reformation.

If this prison prayer, however, is to be a truly reformatory experience, it must be entered into alone. Do not allow your top defense lawyer, the self-justifying side of your personality, to accompany you. Your attorney will insist on preserving your "rights" and will try to whitewash your behavior. Nor should you let a judge be present in your cell. Whenever judges invade your solitude, silence them! Simply sit with your situation in non-judgment. Examine thoroughly the issue to see what it looks and feels like. If it hurts, ask yourself, "Where does it hurt?" Then sit with the pain without attempting to remove it. If you sit with it long enough, the pain will pass. Then you can begin to see that every conflict has roots and that you can trace any wounds back to their beginnings. Sit with your reactions—and with the reactions of others—to what has happened. Sit in stillness as free of judgment and as full of ownership as possible. Strive to see as clearly as possible all sides of the issue. In such silence, you will hear a voice calling you not to self-justification but to self-reformation.

Retreat time or prison prayer further offers us a chance to daily experience life itself. The most precious gift we possess is being alive. Yet we seldom enjoy this gift since we are so caught up with life's problems and so busy with daily activities. Solitude allows us to slow down the rush of life and experience what it means to simply breathe, to see, to hear and think. Solitude allows us time to become conscious of how the mind is forever living in what happened yesterday or what might happen tomorrow. The paradox is that the present moment is perpetually imprisoned because Warden Mind is so restless, so locked into the past or the future, so intent on anything but the "now" moment of life.

Retreat time also offers us an opportunity for conscious silent eating. As prisoners once had to eat in total silence, we might find that solitary meals, eaten without radio, TV or charming conversation with others can free us to discover the vast richness of taste in our food and to discover genuine gratitude. Not only eating but other human activities performed in slow motion can open doors to the fullness of life promised to us by Jesus.

The slang expression, "the old ball and chain," (referring to one's wife or husband as a restriction as confining as the large, black iron ball and chain once fastened to a prisoner's leg) suggests how we can benefit from Prison Prayer. When we voluntarily "ball and chain" ourselves, we are forced to move about at half speed. In such a "retreat walk" we discover the paradoxical truth that when we are prevented from easily escaping the present moment, we are then truly able to experience it. Our actions slowed down, we discover the simple joys that are so easily eclipsed by our energetic style of life. Self-imposed restraints can open our eyes and all our senses to the glory of God, which is nothing less than the presence of the Divine Mystery. Today we tend to smile at one of Henry David Thoreau's concerns about trains. He feared that people would lose their souls, their relationship with nature, if they rode trains traveling at speeds of up to thirty miles an hour! Yet if Thoreau's insight that speed can cause loss of soul is true, then solitude is a way to find it again—and not only find it, but enrich it.

"Fools rush in where angels fear to tread." Throughout history, all the great religious heroes and heroines who achieved mystical union with the Divine Mystery and became aware of their oneness with all, did so by retreating. They sought the kind of solitude that can break down the barriers of conditioned thought and daily habitual living which separate an individual from God.

More than privacy, more than being alone, solitude is a sacred, fertile cell shared with God. Blest are those who have the courage to seek it. Daily personal prayer and meditation and retreat experiences help us to integrate our usually unrelated thoughts and feelings by allowing them an environment in which they can interact. Being in solitude provides space and time to be in touch with our deepest feelings, regrets and thoughts and allows them to reform themselves into new patterns that lead to new forms of behavior. The purpose of any reform is precisely that, a new creative formation of, and within, our very person. It is easy in our crowded, noisy society with its ever present radios, televisions and telephones—and now, even car and portable phones—to lose touch with and become alienated from ourselves and our deepest desires. If we wish to achieve our highest potential, to be mentally and physically healthy, to find the pearl of happiness in this life or to grow in the image of God, then we must frequently escape to the prison of solitude.

The card game Solitaire is one that's played in solitude. Holy Fools play their own game of Solitaire; it's a game played not alone but with God and self. It's a game of the spirit loved by saints. Solitaire, the card game, is known in some countries as Patience. Those foolish enough to waste time alone become aces at patience, a quality so often lacking in today's hurried, instant-response world.

Exercises:

A SOLITARY CONFINEMENT ACTIVITY FOR INNER CONFLICT RESOLUTION

Let's say that you just had an unpleasant encounter with someone whose behavior has upset you. You feel angry at what he or she has done or failed to do. Sentence yourself to about thirty minutes in your private penitentiary of the bedroom or bathroom. Sit down and calm your body by simply being present to the emotion and then allowing it to work itself out of you. Don't force it; just let it slowly pass. Then, when you feel calmer, set a stage within your mind's eye. Place into a chair the person who has upset you. Walk around the person slowly, beginning with the side of that person that has just caused you discomfort. Fully acknowledge that behavior and your reaction to it. Then begin to move around to the positive sides of the person, recalling one by one his or her good points. Take time to experience your reaction to each of the good qualities in turn. When you have completed the circle of the total person and have returned to where you began, with the recent behavior which has caused you pain, you will probably see it in an entirely new light, in the balanced vision of the other's total reality. You can then return to the other or to whatever tasks are at hand, at peace with him or her and with yourself. Or, if you need to, you can go to that person and talk about the conflict from your regained center.

A CANNONBALL MINI-RETREAT

Too busy to go on a retreat? Here's an easy five-minute retreat.

On April 23, 1865, Secretary of War Edwin Stanton ordered four men accused of complicity in the assassination of Abraham Lincoln to be placed in separate cells. Each prisoner had a canvas bag placed over his head with openings only for the eyes and nose. And to each leg was chained a seventy-five pound cannonball!

Go for a brief (about five minutes) walk. Imagine that you are dragging behind each ankle a great seventy-five pound cannonball. Of course, you will walk very slowly with that heavy weight, taking one deliberate step at a time. Let your thoughts be centered only upon the act of walking. Experience the "feel" of your feet touching the earth. Be totally present to what is happening in the present moment, to what you see or hear as you take this Prisoner's Promenade. Then slowly return in the same mindfulness, arriving home refreshed and spiritually renewed.

The Story Continues

I closed the book and reflected. The Master's times away had made this journey a game of solitaire for me. I hadn't minded being alone, at least not as much as I once had. Being alone, and enjoying it, was beginning to grow on me as a pleasant pastime. Patience was something I was slowly also learning from the Master. However, I still felt like a poor beginner as a disciple. While questions stuck to me like burrs to my socks, I was growing used to having them hang on unanswered. Among the many that were stuck to me was the question about who was St. Pantaleone from the Master's prayer last night.

Besides the question burrs, it felt like I was a walking flea circus. Little fears jumped like female fleas all over me. Female fleas, I understand, are more lively than males since they're stronger. I had some very strong little fears. One that I felt leaping around more than the others was the fear that I wouldn't become free enough to be a fool, which the Master seemed to consider extremely important.

I spent some time practicing several of the exercises in the book. I reflected on the events of the previous day and my reactions to them. I hadn't told the Master, but I knew he had guessed that I would have been embarrassed—actually shamed—to have been with him as his disciple when he preached in the village square. I feared flunking the test for my Fool's License if that examination included acting like a buffoon!

Leaning back against a large tree, I found a comfortable position and again opened my book.

The Twin Enemies of Holy Fools

"**W**ho told you that you were naked?**"** is perhaps history's oldest unanswered question. Since God asked the question, it deserves an answer, even if a few millenniums late. "Children, *who* told you that you were naked?" We know that there were no full-length mirrors in Eden, so how did they know they were naked?

After eating the forbidden fruit, "the eyes of both were opened, and they realized that they were naked; so they sewed fig leaves together and made loincloths for themselves" (Gen. 3:7). At sunset, in the breezy time of day when a cool wind blows in off the ocean—as it still does today in Palestine—God took a stroll through the garden. Eden, however, was empty! God wondered, "Is this a game? Are the kids playing hide-and-seek?" Well, they weren't playing a game, but they were hiding. "I was afraid because I was naked," said Adam, "so I hid myself."

The birth of the first twins, Guilt and Shame, is eclipsed by the more dynamic parts of the story, like Adam and Eve being driven out of the garden by an angel with a flaming sword. The angel then took up eternal sentry duty at Eden's gates. Adam was ashamed because he was naked. Shame on Adam! He and Eve covered their nakedness not with fig leaves; rather, they were clothed with shame! You and I know the feel of that Eden garment.

Shame is more painful than any hair shirt. A shame shirt is so painful that we will do almost anything rather than wear it. For example, is not shame the reason we fear speaking in public? Studies show that one thing most people fear more than cancer, snakes, flying or any other terror is speaking in front of others. Yes, we dread that most ancient disease, Edenitis, the fear of being shamed.

The Eden twins, Guilt and Shame, are with us today and daily drive us in various, hidden ways. Forever playing hide-and-seek, when least expected they jump out to grab control of us. When we make a mistake, they hurry us into hiding, saying, "Conceal your error, pretend it didn't happen." When that fails, as it did in Eden, they urge hiding the mistake behind a cluster of fig leaves of excuses, blaming others or uncontrollable circumstances.

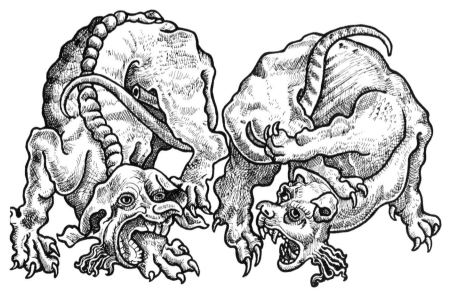

Guilt and Shame operate the world's oldest puppet show. The twins pull invisible wires that cause us to dance to tunes we hate and open our mouths to speak what we detest. Whenever you feel the tug of some invisible puppeteer pulling your strings, pull back! Withdraw from the revolving door of life for a moment, sit quietly and ask, "Who pulled my strings?" Slowly, with care, finger the strings, following them back in time to find their source.

"Who told you that you were naked?" is a haunting question that neither Adam nor Eve answered, and one that we ignore. What is the source of their perception that it was wrong, shameful, to be naked? For Eve and Adam B.A.—Before the Apple—there was no shame in seeing each other naked. Indeed, hadn't they been "made in the image of God"? (The implication of that scriptural quote is delightfully shocking: is God naked?)

Since the Eden twins, Shame and Guilt, are often mistaken for one another, it would be helpful to identify them. Guilt is the painful *fact* of being responsible for an offense or wrongdoing. It is also sometimes used to mean remorse, as in, "I feel guilty about having done that." It is in this latter sense that the two can be confused because shame too is a painful emotion caused by a sense of being guilty.

Shame, however, carries the quality of embarrassment or disgrace. We are familiar with the old expression, "shamefaced," which can mean being bashful. Originally, it meant to be "held fast by shame." That is a fair description of our condition when we are held prisoner by shame. Why do we feel held fast by shame about various parts of the body, about being naked? If that shame is a reflection of a true guilt, what offense has the body committed that we should feel shameful?

The recent restoration of the Sistine Chapel frescoes of Michelangelo, *The Creation* and *The Last Judgment*, had one controversial feature.

The original brilliant colors of the frescoes were revived as centuries of candle smoke and the paint used to repair damage caused by water and time were removed with exacting care. The restoration was not complete, however, since the Vatican chose not to remove certain "touch-ups" made during the Counter Reformation. In the fresco of *The Last Judgment*, it was decided not to remove the loincloths that had been painted in the Sixteenth Century over the naked bodies of the Risen Christ and the Virgin Mary! Shame on the Vatican!

Loincloths painted over naked bodies in Renaissance paintings or marble fig leaves hung on nude statues were part of the Catholic Church's puritanical reaction to the Protestant Reformation. The failure of the Vatican to give permission for the full restoration of Michelangelo's masterpiece to its original state indicates that the Sixteenth Century shadow of shame still hangs over us. Instead of theology influencing art, in this case it has lagged behind. Not only the Vatican but the rest of the Christian Churches seem to have taken up the role of policeman rather than patron of the arts. The art and theology of Christianity should reflect God's vote of approval of creation, the blue ribbon, declaring all of it, "Very good."

Our belief system, our theology, declares that the resurrection of Jesus was the restoration of humanity to its full and former glory as an image of God. To hide as shameful or improper any part of Christ's risen body teaches that certain parts of the human body, even after the Resurrection, are shameful. The fear of the Vatican is understandable—who wants the Sistine Chapel given an "X" rating? Might tourists not come just to gape or giggle at a nude Christ? The problem, however, is not just the Vatican's; it's ours, and it's a problem of our faith and our eyes.

We have eyes that are A.A.—After the Apple! Eve and Adam, B.A.—Before the Apple—whenever they looked at one another, saw beauty, a glorious divine image. Our personal redemption—and that of the world—isn't a restoration that requires waiting until death. Rather, it's a bodily redemption that has already begun. Baptism is not just a spiritual event; it's a wet, chilly bodily experience that is intended to restore us, body and soul. Baptism is both death and birth. It is dying in Christ so as to share—now, in this life, as well as in the next—a new life in the glorious and risen Christ. We die to sin and guilt and so are "de-shamed."

In early Christianity the rite of Baptism required taking off one's shame—as well as all one's clothes—and plunging naked into the waters of the font. Since even at that time people wore shame underneath their underwear, they balked at this ritual nakedness. They were told by the early saints, "Do not be ashamed of your nakedness. By the creative waters of Baptism you have been restored by Christ into God's original design. Do not feel shame, for your guilt has been removed! Your body is now restored to its sacred and original divine design."

While today we echo the theology of the early Christian community, it is often only symbolic, token theology. Do we truly believe that our bodies have been fully restored in Christ? Do our attitudes about our bodies and the bodies of others reveal our faith, or do we still wear shame as our primal garment, our real underwear?

The next time you feel ashamed, ask yourself, "Who told you that you were naked?" Ask, "Who said that you should feel shameful?" If you have committed an offense against another or against God, then shame would be a healthy emotion. Such shame could empower you to seek pardon, to make amends and to reform your life. If no offense is present, however, probe carefully the shame inducing voice you heard. If you ask the question with persistence, you probably will find that its source is an homogenized voice, a chorus that rises from your childhood.

This voice of "conscience" is a collection of voices belonging to parents, classmates, childhood enemies, teachers and preachers, which has given shape to early fears and feelings of being inferior. Entwined

within this chorus' various accents are the voices of society, culture and lifestyles that are in vogue. A good conscience, on the other hand, is an essential ally on the spirit path since it helps us judge between good, appropriate shame and inappropriate, unjustified shame. Good shame is essential for creative holiness and positive growth. Yet some people feel more ashamed for picking their noses in public than for making racial slurs. Others burn with shame when they mispronounce a word but feel nothing when blindly walking past a homeless person.

Whenever you feel the itchy pain of shame's undershirt, ask, "Who told you that you were fat, short, skinny?…Who told you that you were dumb and would never amount to anything?…Who told you that you were bad, unwanted, unworthy?…Who told you that you were not lovable?"

Shame can be a subterranean lurking in the cellar of our hearts. Like buried toxic trash, shame from childhood fears or some long-forgotten dark deed (committed perhaps when the difference between right and wrong was limited) can seep upward, poisoning daily life. Subterranean shame is constantly restless, anxious to be connected to some specific offense. In some people it escapes the cellar frequently for "one-night stands" so it can find rest in being connected to some shameful deed. Other people send mirrors on long strings into the cellars of their hearts so their shame can be reflected outward. The distorted image of their shame is then projected upon others, upon works of art or theater, all of which are denounced as, "dirty, filthy and shameful!"

"Who told you that you were naked?" An answer could be, "My conscience!" The challenge at the dawn of a new millennium is to find true freedom of conscience. This involves a rejection of the simple solution of letting others determine for you what is morally right or wrong. Mature spirituality requires entering faith's fiery furnace to forge your own contemporary conscience. Such a conscience involves more than sexual morality; it includes social, ecological and political issues. The Second Vatican Council declared a generation ago that "...only in freedom can people direct themselves towards goodness...authentic freedom is an exceptional sign of the divine image within humanity..." (*Church in the Modern World*). "This Vatican Council declares that the human person has the right to religious freedom...that in religious matters no one is forced to act in a manner contrary to his or her beliefs..." (*Declaration on Religious Freedom*).

True conscience, the Spirit's guiding voice, is constantly being formed by a prayerful reflection on the teachings of the Gospel, the wisdom of the Church and past ages, and God's voice heard within your own heart. True freedom of conscience requires the silent prayer of listening as an integral part of the process. It also can be aided by an honest consultation with someone qualified in such matters. Then, when the many voices in your heart harmonize into a healthy, holy and single voice, have the courage to follow it—regardless of how it might first sound. That voice is more than a barometer of conscience about what is right or wrong, it is a radio beacon intended to bring you Home.

That voice of true conscience is an alarm clock gently awakening you to live in the wholesome beauty of all God's creation—and in freedom and love. It reminds you, regardless of what you may have heard in church or in old childhood tapes, that at the end of each day of creation God looked upon what had been created and said, "Hmmm, that's Good!"

Exercises:

AN EXERCISE FOR DE-SHAMING YOURSELF

Shameful feelings can be created by tapes of old authority voices that play over and over in our minds. Make new tapes and play them frequently. For example, since we are frequently ashamed of our  bodies, you could make this tape: "My body is beautiful and I'm proud of it." Repeat this daily as you bathe, dress or look in the mirror. An allied exercise would be to erase thoughts that support feelings of being ashamed of yourself, such as, "If only I weighed thirty pounds less...were three inches taller...had more hair...."

AN EXERCISE FOR DE-SHAMING OTHERS

Making mistakes in life is a sign of our humanity. No one is exempt from errors; we make them daily. When someone makes a mistake in which you are involved as the responsible person—as a parent, leader or manager—here's a novel and potentially enriching exercise. Take responsibility for that person's mistake! Say to the child or employee, "I am responsible for this error; I should have make it clearer to you what I wanted done," or "If I had given you a note about it, you wouldn't have forgotten. It's my fault." Such partnership in mistakes makes errors less shameful and easier to own—and prevents unnecessary shaming.

How to Play Lifeball

The clown, jester and fool made a game out of life. With laughter, they invited others to enter that sacred, zany zone called "play." In today's hectic world, most people find themselves bankrupt of time. When we're busy, the first two things we jettison overboard from our busy schedules are prayer and play. Play is non-productive activity; not even exercise or weight loss can be the object of true play. The paradox is that only unwise fools abandon play or prayer.

Stress, the arch-enemy of prayerful play, is not so much caused by overwork, by approaching deadlines or long lines at check-out stands. Stress, that source of heart attacks and vicious verbal attacks, is caused more by interior than exterior conditions. It is not the traffic jam at the bathroom door or on the expressway that makes you and me stressful; it's our thoughts about those conflicts.

Life has always been full of stress. To stand erect, as our ancient ancestors first learned, places us in a natural stress zone. It compels us to pull ourselves upward against the downward drag of earth's gravity. As infants we learned to balance the kind of stress created by these opposite forces. We first learned how to crawl, then to pull ourselves upright with the aid of a table or chair. A short time later, to the applause of family and friends, we were able to walk without falling down as a victim of gravity. That initial simple stress balancing act is something we now take for granted.

A special kind of stress is the subject of this chapter. When they are learning to balance gravity's stress in the art of walking, small children seem to delight in the challenge. Perhaps there's a secret in that for us stress-conscious adults. The solution to one form of High Stress Syndrome is hidden in a new ball game called *Lifeball*! Like all games, it's educational play. In addition, Lifeball can be played anywhere, and it requires no special equipment or uniforms (though many teams choose to wear distinctive dress).

In Lifeball, players are divided into two teams, each with an equal number of male and female members. Any kind of object may be used as the playing ball as long as it can be easily carried: pots, pans, a briefcase, etc. While the rules of the game combine those of baseball, football and basketball, there are some minor differences.

Five of these rule variations are:

1. In Lifeball, the rules of the game can be changed at any time but only by a team that is at least 20 points ahead.

2. Cheating is permitted and encouraged if it is cleverly done. No player is punished for cheating as long as that player crosses the goal line and scores. If a player cheats but fails to score, that player's team is penalized—often severely.

3. Referees are required to penalize all violations of rules by the losing team but are not obliged to do so to the winning team. That decision is left up to the officials.

4. While both Lifeball teams are half women and half men, the women are not allowed to call game plays or to score points. If a female player should receive a pass, she must in turn pass the (object) ball to a male player who will then score the winning point.

5. If a player of one team is running for the goal line and no player of the opposing team is close enough to catch him, Clause #3-F can be employed. Clause #3-F, the "Fan Clause," states that any loyal fan of the opposing team can jump from the stands and onto the field to tackle a player as long as no player of the fan's team is available. This Fan Clause is akin to a citizen's arrest in civil law.

I can hear you saying to yourself, "Lifeball not only sounds like a game for clowns, it isn't fair!" Ah, that's what makes it such a great game—it's so educational. Sports are considered an integral part of our schooling since they teach youth about teamwork and life values. Lifeball—unlike other sports which require that all rules be observed and the game be played fairly—teaches that life *isn't* fair! Since real life is more unfair than fair, Lifeball is a tremendous learning tool.

It was our childhood play that planted the acorn idea in our minds that "life is supposed to be fair." That enshrined thought has become a sacred oak in the middle of our minds. This one idea is the source of much of our "dis-stress." Don't you feel the fires of anger rise inside at injustice in our legal system, cheating in the marketplace—and unfairness in the way you're treated? What's really disturbing is that not only is life not fair, God isn't fair either!

Who would list as his or her favorite parable of Jesus the one about the vineyard workers? The God that Jesus casts as the owner of the vineyard is an unfair God! Recall the parable: The owner goes at dawn into the village square and hires workers for the usual daily wage. Again at midmorning, noon and mid-afternoon he goes to hire more workers. Finally, very late in the afternoon he returns to the square and hires additional workers. An hour later at sunset he instructs his foreman to pay the workers. When the last to be hired—those who only worked one hour—are paid the same wages as those who had labored all day, a labor dispute erupts. "Not fair! Unjust!" shout those hired at dawn. "How can those who worked only one hour be given the same wages as us who have labored all day under the hot sun!" (See Mt. 20: 1-16).

The UGPU, Union of Grape Pickers United, would stage a strike today against any company with such "unfair" labor practices. The UGPU would set up a picket line at the gate of such a vineyard, and wouldn't many good, righteous people join in the demonstration? The implications of that parable, if you reflect on it, are truly disturbing— if not stressful. It just isn't fair that God would give the same reward to those who have been good only one hour—their last hour on earth— as to those who have been faithful their entire lives! It just isn't fair!

It's easy to identify with those angry, weary grape pickers in the parable. Reflect for a moment on this modern parallel parable: A typical, upright hard worker is driving home in rush-hour traffic. One after another on the side of the highway are large orange signs that read, "Left Lane Closed Ahead." Our hard worker promptly directs his car into the right lane. From behind him, one by one, other drivers do the same. There is a long, single line of slow moving vehicles, leaving the left lane empty. Suddenly a few drivers speed past in the left lane, racing toward the front of the line. They continue until they come to the barricade with its large flashing arrow, where they squeeze into the lane of traffic. As they do, our hard worker feels the pilot light flare up under his age-old idea about "fairness," igniting his anger. "That's not fair, you're cheating!" His resentment finds expression as he bumper-to-bumpers his car with the one in front so as not to allow another cheater to slip into line ahead of him. Such "unfair" behavior creates a storm within him. His nervous system is drenched with primitive behavior juices, causing him to grip the steering wheel as if it were a weapon. Who among us does not relate to this experience?

The good, never-left-the-farm brother in the prodigal son parable never drove in rush-hour traffic, yet he too felt that sense of anger and injustice. His was the same anger as that of the weary grape pickers. What is even more disturbing and stressful is that this theme of God rewarding those who do not qualify for a reward is often repeated in the Gospels. Jesus, for example, in the last moments of his life, rewards with heaven a criminal crucified next to him for one statement of affirmation after a whole life of crime! Really now, is that fair?

What fuels the anger of the good brother of the prodigal, the tired grape pickers and of you and me as we respond to milder forms of injustice in our lives? Is it not, to a great degree, envy? Like dry tinder, envy feeds the flame of anger. Envy is the bastard child of comparison, and nothing is so destructive as comparing oneself to others. Because comparison gives birth to envy, we must be cautious. Who knows, maybe the presence or absence of envy in our hearts may be life's last Big Exam?

After a lifelong struggle to obey the commandments, play fair, be honest and just, loving and faithful, we might find that the feast of heaven is a surprise party! Consider for a moment how you might respond if the seating at God's eternal Easter banquet is a bit unusual. What if directly across from you is Saint Adolph Hitler; on his left is Saint Francis of Assisi; and on his right, St. Joseph Stalin? Picture in the chair to your left a transvestite who looks like Marilyn Monroe; to your right is Mother Theresa of Calcutta; on her right is a maker of children's porno films!

If left unchallenged in this lifetime, that strongly planted idea that life is supposed to be fair may generate feelings of stress and resentment that last into the next life! It wouldn't be fair, but it might be just like God to test us by watching how we respond when we find our companions in the next life to be last-minute reformed rapists, murderers and villains of all sorts. Will we resent—or rejoice in— God's great love that made it possible for some to enter Paradise because with their last breath they whispered, "Oh, God, I'm sorry"?

Jesus is the incarnation of the love of God. In our passion for justice we can easily forget that. The prophets and Jesus called us to work for justice, equal justice for all. How can one be called a disciple of Jesus and turn one's back on injustice in society or the Church? However, while we struggle for justice and equality for all, regardless of race, religion, sex or sexual preference, let us not presume that God will act "fair and square." God's love is not determined in a just way, at least as we consider justice. It is rather a gift. God's love cannot be earned or merited. It is given mysteriously and always as an unconditional gift.

We love in a Godlike way when we attempt to love others whether or not they play by the rules of the game. Love, like any game, has its rules. In love's Lifeball rule book are found a couple of interesting regulations: "You want me to respect you, then you must be respectable!" and "Don't get out of line!" That one-liner brings us back to the rush-hour conflict with drivers who don't play fair.

The car on my left is trying to squeeze into my lane of traffic. Its front right blinker is on as it noses over to cut in. What's my response? If I'm trying to be Godlike, shouldn't I first give the driver a big, friendly grin? Next, I give my love some physical expression as I brake and wave a signal to cut in ahead of me. You may ask, "Why encourage such nasty driving habits and rude behavior?" My response is based not on my desire to deal with another's bad habits but with mine! It can be an exercise in removing the bad habits of comparison and judgment of others.

Perhaps the very act of reading such a response has been stressful for you. If it seems too radical or raises too many red victim flags in your mind, then maybe you should come up with a solution that suits you! Sit with the dilemma, talk it over with friends, pray with it. But as you do, remember Jesus' call to perfection in St. Matthew's Gospel: "Offer no resistance to injury...if anyone wants your shirt, hand over your coat as well. Should anyone press you into service for one mile, go two miles" (Mt. 5: 39-41). It seems that Jesus' way involves giving up your space in line, if not a whole extra mile.

If I don't compare *my rights* in rush-hour traffic to another's, then I don't have to share my front seat with a horrible hitchhiker: Envy! There may be a good reason for the driver's hurry: maybe she's late for an appointment; maybe his wife is having a baby. By not reacting to the "implant" thought that life should be fair, I can be generous with my time as well as my place in line.

While I try to act like and love like God, I'm not God. I don't know the driver's motives, but I give a love-gift of ascribing to him/her the best of motives. I don't know if indeed I'm encouraging bad behavior in others, but I do know that I'm encouraging the good behavior of non-judgment and non-comparison in myself. I also know that as I strive to change old, deeply rooted thoughts, I am drastically decreasing life's stress as I increase my capacity to enjoy life.

Want to be free of stress? Then discipline yourself to take time to sit and observe the kind of thoughts you entertain. If you discover that the behavior of others makes you angry, it would be well to see if your anger is the result of ancient dogmatic ideas like, "Everyone should always play fair." In the process of becoming adults, we acquire a long list of incorrect assumptions that easily become the source of suffering and stress in our lives.

One by one, cleanse your mind of such thoughts that only create stress. In their place, cultivate the enjoyment of life. As you cleanse yourself of assumptions, replace them with thoughts like, "Never judge another" or "Never compare yourself to others." Whenever you can eliminate the stress created by certain unreal thoughts, you can begin to enjoy the delight of natural stressful living!

Running and dancing are a couple of ways of enjoying the natural stress between the planet's magnetic pull and your abilities to stretch beyond it. Or you can enjoy good old ordinary walking. If you can remember the sheer delight of your first unassisted walk as a small child, then walking can be play, pleasure and prayer. But, you know what? It just isn't fair that some folks get so much enjoyment out of life while the majority have to work and suffer!

Reflections and Exercises:

FOR MY THOUGHTS ARE NOT YOUR THOUGHTS, NOR ARE YOUR WAYS MY WAYS. AS HIGH AS THE HEAVENS ARE ABOVE THE EARTH, SO HIGH ARE MY WAYS ABOVE YOUR WAYS AND MY THOUGHTS ABOVE YOUR THOUGHTS.

Prophet Isaiah, 55: 8-9

A LIST OF ENTRENCHED THOUGHTS THAT PRODUCE STRESS

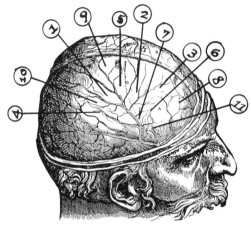

1. People have no right to talk in picture theaters.
2. Each time I come to bat I should hit a home run.
3. It's a mortal sin to be late.
4. There's no justice in the Church when women can't be ordained.
5. It's not fair that people who smoke can't do so in "public" places.
6. A good day is a day in which nothing goes wrong.
7. It's shameful to make a mistake.
8. It's not fair to those trying to worship when parents keep crying babies in church.
9. People should carry their own weight.
10. I'm the only one who can do "it."
11. I shouldn't think stressful thoughts.

BRAIN BABY-SITTING

Frequently our thoughts behave like spoiled children. Instead of attempting to eject thoughts that create anger and distress, you might learn to sit with them like a baby sitter.

Explore the internal conflict to find the idea that gave rise to it...just sit with it lovingly. Don't judge it, just observe it. This "baby-sitting" will make you more conscious of your unconscious seed thoughts.

When you are peacefully aware of the source of what disturbs you, you can act to replace it with another thought that's more in line with reality—and with who you want to be.

MIND LAUNDRY

As it is necessary to frequently launder our clothes, so we must be zealous in the frequent laundering of our thoughts. Here are five simple Mind Laundry suggestions:

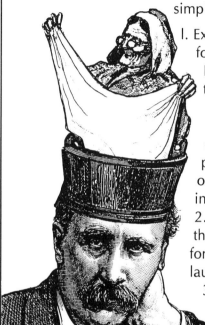

1. Examine thoughts as you do clothing for signs of a need to launder them. Examples of "dirty" thoughts are those that (a) turn on your pilot light which ignites the fires of anger, (b) cause you to be depressed, overburdened or stressful, (c) contain the echoes of parental figures saying, "should... ought...have to...," (d) make you feel inadequate, inferior or ashamed.

2. Take care, for deeply stained thoughts may have to soak in silence for some minutes before you attempt to launder them.

3. Acknowledge that some thoughts will not become free of stain without frequent washings.

4. Be gentle as you clean your thoughts. Avoid harsh cleansing solutions or instant Remove All Dirt products offered by slick-talking salespersons. Always launder your thoughts with gentle, loving care.

5. Freshly laundered thoughts will dry best when they are hung outdoors and exposed to natural light and air.

KEEP UP APPEARANCES; THERE LIES THE TEST; THE WORLD WILL GIVE THEE CREDIT FOR THE REST. OUTWARD BE FAIR, HOWEVER FOUL WITHIN; SIN IF THOU WILT, BUT THEN IN SECRET SIN.

Charles Churchhill, 1731-1764

The Story's End
Becomes the Beginning

"You get a gold star, Nipper! I caught you studying! Looks like you've almost finished your handbook." He was leaning over my shoulder and had startled me with his surprise appearance.

"Master, welcome back! I'm glad you've returned. I didn't hear you coming. I guess I was caught up in learning how to play the game of Lifeball. And, yes, I'm just about to read the last couple of pages of the handbook."

"I hope you had a good night's sleep. I'm curious, did you dream about lightning and thunderbirds? If you did, then you woke up as a heyoka!"

"No, I can't recall any dreams. But what's a heyoka?" I asked.

"A Native American Indian clown, trickster and fool. They're very valuable in the tribe because the thunder-beings, the gods, command them to act in a silly way. They're more valuable than money because heyokas protect the people from lightning and thunderstorms. Their laughter is always seen as holy, very sacred.

"Perhaps tomorrow night you'll dream of lightning and thunderbirds and wake up as a heyoka. For now, gather up our things. It's time for us two fools to get back on the Yellow Brick Road again," he said as he picked up his bedroll.

We shouldered our few belongings and began walking through the forest. I had lost my sense of direction by this time and wasn't sure just where we were headed. The Master apparently did, however, so I faithfully followed him. After a short while, a narrow path slowly took shape. It twisted through the maze of trees wide enough that we were able to walk side-by-side. I took the occasion to ask, "Master, did you enjoy your visit with your hermit friend?"

"I did, but it wasn't a visit. We spend most of the time just sitting together in silence. Occasionally we take turns interrupting the silence to tell the other a joke. Then we share holy community by laughing.

"He told me about this Jewish woman raised in the liberal leftist tradition who was part of a socialist movement in her youth. She wasn't a practicing Jew; in fact, she was more an atheist. Well, one day she takes her grandson to the beach. He's her favorite. She buys him a little yellow sun hat, a swim suit, a sand pail and shovel. As he plays in the sand, she falls asleep in her beach chair. The little boy wanders out into the surf and is caught up in an undertow. The boy begins screaming as he's being pulled out to sea. The woman wakes up and yells, 'Save my child,' only to see that the sun is setting and everyone else on the beach has gone home.

"Atheist or not, she starts screaming to high heaven, 'Please, God, save my child! Creator of the Universe, blest be Thou, I promise that if you save my grandchild, little Abraham, I will go to the synagogue every Saturday. I will eat only Kosher food. I'll do anything! Just save my grandchild.' Sure enough, the child is tossed safely up on the shore. She runs down, bends over the child and sees that he is breathing. Then she frowns, and pointing a finger up to heaven she demands, 'He had a *hat*!'

"So the two of us laughed and laughed, and then we sat in silence for another half an hour. At that point I said to him, 'The Rumanians say that before you find God, you are eaten by the saints.' And he says to me, 'As the Fulani of Africa say, God will not drive flies away from a tailless cow.' This time we chuckled before diving back into silence.

"Then I said, 'I understand that Ramakrishna said that a perfect knower of God and a perfect idiot have the same outer signs: each laughs, weeps, dances and sings. Sometimes they behave like a child—guileless, generous, without vanity, unattached to anything, always blissful.'

"My friend smiled and said, 'Ah, yes, like Mullah Nassr Eddin in the Muslim Persian tradition, or as he was elsewhere known, Nasruddin Hodja—Hodja meaning wise teacher. Well, one day the Hodja was relaxing under a walnut tree. He began to speculate on how strange it was that Allah had made such small walnuts grow on such a large tree, while large pumpkins in a nearby patch were growing on insignificant little vines. "How strange your ways, Allah," he sighed. "What could be sillier than tiny things growing on a big tree, and huge things growing on tiny vines?" At that very moment a walnut fell on the Hodja's head leaving a painful bump. He jumped to his feet, raised his face to heaven and prayed, "Allah, O Allah, I am a fool and you are wise; where would I be now if pumpkins grew on trees?" ' Both of us laughed ourselves into silence."

The Master said nothing more, and the two us walked on in silence. As we walked, I pondered about these jokes and stories and their place in sacred instruction. I also wondered: if you truly became holy, had true knowledge of God, would you then also, as Ramakrishna said, be a perfect idiot! Maybe I was an idiot. At least I felt stupid—not because of holiness but because I struggled to understand why the Master and his hermit friend spent their time with silence and laughter. Silence and holy conversation I could understand, but laughter?

The Master, as always, guessed what I was thinking. Turning toward me with a look of great affection, he said, "Silence and laughter together give one a rare, exotic and intoxicating sip of paradise. Some say that heaven is the perfect mixture of music and silence. Others teach that the best blend is making love and silence. Perhaps it's all these happening simultaneously."

"But isn't the world filled with evil?" I asked. "Child abuse, sexual violence, the most horrible oppression—how can any sane person laugh and tell jokes? You've made fun of churches for being so lacking in joy, but how can they be places of mirth and clowning when they're surrounded by such darkness and evil?"

"Nipper, George Bernard Shaw said it so well, 'That older and greater church to which I belong: the church where the oftener you laugh the better, because by laughter only can you destroy evil without malice.' Whenever evil is fought with malice, the result is an even deeper evil! In spirituality, when even worship is devoid of laughter and joy, the sacred circle is broken. Among the Native Americans of the Northwest, certain rites and sacred ceremonies can't begin until the guests start to laugh! They believe that only after you have started to laugh is the inner ground prepared to enter the sacred dimensions.

"It's a sad reality, but what's happened to art and life has also affected clowning and humor. Modern art is generally restricted to art galleries and museums. In the same way, clowning largely has been removed from daily life and limited to the theater or television. Whenever popes and patriarchs, bishops and church elders, mullahs and ministers, or any religious leaders cannot bear to be the butt of a joke or jest, it's a sign that they suffer from consecrated constipation. When they are so respectable as to be beyond humor, then they have lost humility, the mother of holiness."

Again, the only sound was the wind moving the tops of the trees as the Master and I walked along the narrow forest path in silence. This time the period of silence was much longer than before. As I walked in silent step with him, I felt a hunch creeping over me. An intuition whispered to me that my time with the Master was about to end. I couldn't explain it logically; I simply knew that the fateful hour was upon us. I looked at him and knew that, while our time together had not been very long, I had grown to love this unconventional, eccentric holy man. I felt as well that I had learned far more than I thought I had, even if I wasn't yet able to explain my new understanding. His radar being so sensitive, he stopped walking and winked at me.

"Since you've finished all but the last pages of the book, I think it's time for you to take your examination. Tell me what you've learned."

I paused for an uncertain moment; then the words began to roll out. "I've learned that to balance on the razor-sharp edge of the Way, you must walk like this." I began to walk ahead of him, zig-zagging from one side of the path to the other. "You must learn to be as agile as an acrobat, not leaning too far to the right or the left, never rigid, always elastic."

"You earn another gold star. That's correct, Nipper, but explain," he grinned.

"While sanctity is serious business," I said as I zig-zagged to the other side of the path, "you must court the clown, the inner-jester or the ageless child within to avoid making a rigid religion out of the Way, since it appears so crazy to the practical standards of society." Then swinging to the other side of the path, I went on, "While never misunderstanding the power of the diabolic," and here I did a comical somersault in the middle of the path, "you must practice the madness of Jesus whose very relatives wanted to put him away."

"Another gold star! You know, I believe that last night you dreamt about lightning and thunderbirds! You're acting like a heyoka!" he said, applauding as I danced quickly to the opposite side of the path. "You're walking the narrow edge like a champion, but tell me more."

"Of all the scary boogie-men, Old Death is the worst, so never let Death catch you napping." Making a funny face, I stuck out my tongue, "And those on the Way have fun making fun of Death. They also greet each sunrise as a good day to die, truly welcoming a new day and not a dull encore of yesterday. Faced with freshness, their most frequent expression is, 'thank you.' " Zig-zagging, I continued, "But they never say, 'Thank you' as a door-closer. They find a way to pass on the gift of life, or any gift, by giving of themselves, a la Mafioso."

Ducking behind a tree, I went on, "To escape the old *rigor mortis* caused by overwork and keeping your nose to the grindstone, you must zag to your hidden hermitage lest you become a zombie, one of the living dead." Here, with a leap in the air and a whistle, I jumped to the other side of the path, saying, "and watch out for *wundersucht*."

"*Saltum et siffetum*...but no fart?" he giggled.

Leaping and dancing along, I began singing, "It's a big, wide, wonderful world we live in. There are millions of miracles in life without end." I continued jumping from lesson to lesson, zig-zagging back and forth from one side of the Way to the other, regardless of how difficult the jump. I was truly having fun dancing on the razor's edge. The seeming contradictions of the various chapters were sewn together in my weaving from side to side. It occurred to me that one chapter's lesson was only half of a paradox which was balanced and completed by the following chapter. In the beginning the Master had warned me to beware of a hunger for miracles, and yet here I was in the middle of a miracle!

All the while the Master laughed, applauded and wept with joy. I amazed myself. I was as surprised as he. I couldn't believe how easy I found it, once I let go, to play the fool, even with such holy subjects. Then I heard, very faintly at first, then more clearly, the sound of the river!

Within minutes we made our way out of the dense growth of trees. To my surprise we were at the big bend of the river where I had first met the Master. We stood almost at the very spot. I felt a mixture of emotions. There was great joy at my newfound freedom and how I had been able to dance out what I had learned from the Master. My heart was also saddened to see the rushing river, knowing that, if we had returned to the beginning, then this had to be the end!

The Master swung down his old, white canvas bag from his shoulder. "Ready, Nipper, for your final exam? You've finished the book, you zigged and zagged like an accomplished fool, but there's one more test. It's time for me to go. Feel it? The season's changing, time for me to head back up into the mountains to my hermitage. It's also time for you to return home and become the parish fool. Well, friend, think you're ready for your final exam?"

"I have a hunch—in fact, I've been having a lot of them recently— that this isn't going to be a multiple-choice test. Ready or not, I'm willing to give it a try, on one condition. Like other professional exams, if I flunk this one, can I try again at a later date? If I don't make the grade, can I meet you here by the big bend in the river next season?"

"Sounds only fair to me," he said. "And you're right, this isn't your usual final examination." Reaching into his canvas bag, he removed a baggy pair of colorfully patched pants with bright red fireman-type suspenders. "Slip this pair of pants on, Nipper, and see if they fit. May the all merciful saint be with you."

Slightly embarrassed, I stepped out of my own pants. I pulled the baggy patched pants up to my waist. They were so large that three of me could fit inside of them. I slipped the red suspenders over my shoulders and noticed that on the left suspender was a red, white and blue ribbon. A large gold medal dangled from the ribbon with the word "Hero" in the center of it. It all seemed simple enough, so I asked, "Well, did I pass?"

"Pull on your gold Hero medal," he said, seating himself on the ground.

I gave the gold medal a jerk, and instantly the suspender snaps flew open, causing the baggy pants to drop suddenly around my ankles. My face flashed neon red. I reached down and tried to pull the pants up to my waist again, but in the complicated mass of cloth I couldn't find the tops to the pants. The more I struggled to get them up, the more they became entangled. All the while, the Master rolled on the ground with laughter.

I felt silly standing in front of him without my pants, embarrassed, ashamed. Then, in a flash, I remembered! I saw myself as I truly was, naked, comical and yet lovable. I too began to laugh. Soon the forest echoed with our laughter. It seemed that even the river was giggling with us.

Finally he said, "You've passed the test, Nipper!" Standing up, he reached down into his canvas bag and pulled out his black top hat. Placing it on his head with great ceremony, he stood in front of me. "By the authority invested in me by the Divine Comedy, by the Fraternal Order of Mad Hatters, Clowns and Jesters, by the Silly Sisterhood of Fools and Wise Idiots, I solemnly present you with your Fool's License. May St. Pantaleone intercede for you with the Communion of Holy Fools, the Saints, and bless your zig-zag journey on the razor's edge of the Way." Then like a French general, he kissed me on both cheeks and handed me my certificate. "Remember, Nipper the Fool, that regardless of what happens, 'the show must go on!'

"That's circus talk, you know. As a *holy fool* you must know that the best way to keep your balance—so that the outward person and the inward person are the same, as Plato, or was it Pluto, said—is to fall off the edge!"

"Master," I moaned, "I thought that the purpose of all this training is to be able to walk the razor's edge of the Way without slipping and falling?"

"True, indeed, Nipper! But as that wise Greek philosopher Plato said, 'Love is a rare kind of madness, a divine madness'! Moses and Jesus both called us to God's great commandment: to love God with all your heart and to love your neighbor as yourself. To be faithful to that command is not to slip into love but to fall madly into madness as you fall in love. That wholehearted love of God, self and neighbor *is* the Way. Most people, however, are fearful that if they were to love with such a totality of themselves they would appear mad. And so they *discreetly* love God. Religion, paradoxically, allows for that compromise. But discipleship does not!"

"Isn't love blind? And if I'm blinded by love, will I not fall off the edge?"

"No, love is not blind! The world is blind! Love heals our eyes so that we can see others—and life—with a godly vision. In a world of the blind, such sacred vision is regarded as demented. Those fools, however, who love God with all their hearts see what is really of value in a world where what is valued is really trash. The result of such wide-eyed vision, Nipper, is to appear to have the eyes of a lunatic—like old Putai whom you read about in the first chapter of your manual. Perpetually falling in love, my friend, is the only way to faithfully walk the narrow Way. Even if always being in love makes you a perpetual fool, it's the only way to truly keep your balance."

My heart exploded with happiness! Gone was my embarrassment about not having any pants on. It was so funny to be decorated like a war hero without my pants! Giggling through it all, I couldn't resist asking one more question, "Master, who was St. Pantaleone?"

"To begin with he's the only saint who has loaned his name to an article of clothing—pants! St. Pantaleone was a Fourth Century physician and martyr. He was known as 'all merciful,' a beautiful name, if you ask me, for any physician. Poor saintly Pantaleone was beheaded by the emperor Diocletian. No one can explain why, but this kindly and holy physician somehow passed into Italian folklore as a lovable, simple-minded buffoon. Perhaps, like Jesus and the other true saints, he simply appeared to be simpleminded for losing his head over

Christ. Anyway, as a clown in Italian comedy his character's behavior was anything but saintly. He was depicted as running after women in a crazy way, and just plain acting silly. Pantaleone's stage costume, by which he was instantly recognized, was a pair of very large trousers, tight from the ankle to the knee, then flaring out like giant balloons. Traveling comic actors carried the character of foolish Pantaleone to France and then to England, where both his baggy trousers and the character had the same name: Pantaloon. And, Nipper, that's how we got our name for pants!"

"Interesting, but why pray to him? Don't tell me, I just got it. He lost his head because of his love of God and Christ, right? And losing one's head, as our friend Mother Abbess paradoxically promoted, losing one's logical, rational reasoning about God and the Way, is the secret of finding it. I get it! You must be willing to be a martyr at the hands of the world's or the Church's Diocletians, and be willing to lose your head to find your heart!"

"Another 'A,' Nipper! You're a star student. Yes, it's the heart and the soul that understand mysteries which are beyond the mind. Yet we often place more value on the mind's judgments than those of the heart. Wise are those who know that wisdom is of the heart."

"Master, the asses' ears! I now understand the asses' ears worn by the early Franciscans on their hoods. They were the kind of ears Jesus called his disciples to have. Those who hear God's word and live it out will appear to be as stupid as an ass. I was blind, Master, to your silly and bizarre behavior, failed to see it all as a living parable. Finally I'm beginning to get a glimpse of what you were attempting to teach me. You were not inviting me to be some kind of circus clown, to be a part-time entertainer, but rather to walk the razor's edge of the Way. To do that with integrity and wholeheartedness will make one appear clown-ish, even insane and...."

"Nipper, to walk the narrow razor's edge in a world that's mad does make one appear to be mad. Recall in the early part of your handbook how Jesus' call to love one's enemies, to give up one's riches and become a humble servant to others, to pray always and to love God with a full heart have ever been regarded as madness. Recall too how Jesus was a prisoner before Pilate and the Jewish religious court. It was not Jesus who was really on trial. Rather it was Pilate, Rome and the religious establishment. All of them were judged to be no longer valid, judged to be powerless since a new era had arrived: God's Age. Jesus, the Clown King, mocked by soldiers and priests, was a hanging judge. He granted pardon to all who had judged and crucified."

Then the Master handed me what appeared to be a playing card and said, "Here, this is my favorite holy joker card; I want you to have it. Jesus, wearing his holy foolscap, his crown of thorns, forgave his executioners as being temporarily insane when he said, 'Father, forgive them for they know not what they are doing.' Today, too, those who attempt to resolve problems with power, those who believe that they can act in God's name to block the work of God, are really the insane. War, abuse of power, any kind of eye-for-an-eye—who knows, perhaps all sin, Nipper—is a form of temporary insanity!

"But exercise great caution, my good friend. Remember how thin is the edge of the Way! Hobbyhorse Holiness is not to be romanticized into a fake madness. Nor is it to treat lightly those burdened with true mental problems—which is truly a terrible cross. Make no mistake, Nipper; it's a thin line—I mean the line that separates those who in their minds suffer a perpetual Calvary and those who, by taking seriously the words of Jesus and the other great souls, abandon the values of this world to find liberation. Because the line is too fine, in former times the insane were often viewed as prophets of God—and prophets as insane."

"I think I understand, Master. I also realize now how all the clowning—the hobbyhorse, your crazy top hat and all your tricks— were meant to awaken me to how I would be seen by my family and friends *if* I were to truly seek to be holy and Godlike. Yes, the mud is settling slowly in the pond of my mind. It's becoming clear. The ultimate paradox is that it's not the *holy* fool—notice, Master, how I make that distinction—who is crazy. Rather, it is the world with its crazy creed that wealth and power bring happiness and are more important than love. To live without anxiety, as carefree as the birds of the sky yet concerned about tomorrow, is to balance on the thin edge of the razor. To have the strength to strike a return blow against one who has attacked you or to be clever enough to throw back a more stinging insult—and yet to refrain from either, as Jesus urged, is to appear to be the village dunce! Yet, in all such instances, true wisdom is folly."

I stood beside the rushing river, my baggy clown pants around my feet, as he applauded loudly. It was weird, but I felt so proud standing there without my pants on, yet dressed in insight about one of the great secrets of holiness. I brought my Fool's License to my lips and gave it a big smack. The Master helped me step out of the baggy outfit at my feet and into my old pants. As he did, he looked over my right shoulder upward into the sky. "And, there's one for you too!"

I turned, looking over my right shoulder. "To whom are you speaking, Master?" I said, seeing nothing but sky behind and above me.

"I'm talking to *that* person up there, Nipper, the one who has been reading the *HOLY FOOLS* book over your shoulder all this time. Did you think we were alone?

"Yes, I'm speaking to you up there."

"Who me?"

"Yes, I'm speaking to you, the reader. You've faithfully read the same chapters as Nipper, or you wouldn't be here with us now. So, having also completed the course, you are entitled to a Fool's License. Of course, that is, if you want a license and are ready to be a fool. Many are those who learn how but are afraid to practice the secret knowledge they've learned. If you're willing to be a fool for Christ's sake, then you are worthy to have your Fool's License.

"When you've finished reading this page—no, don't peek. I said, when you're finished, you can turn the page where you will find your very own personal Fool's License, signed by me personally." The Master placed his hands on my shoulders again and winked at me. Then, looking up over my right shoulder, he winked a second time at whoever was up there.

"Is it time, Master, to say good-bye?" I asked.

"No! In fact, friend, it never shall be! It would be impolite to say good-bye, just as it is for the Tanga of Melanesia. At Tanga feasts, dinner guests who have finished eating leave with a simple word to acknowledge the host or other guests. They do not say good-bye because the feasting never stops! To utter such finalizing words suggests that not only the feast, but society and even life itself might just possibly come to an end. Friends and lovers should never say good-bye since the feast of friendship should never die out. Ours is no different. Both of us shall continue to feast even if we are not physically walking together as we have been."

I understood and nodded my head. A slight mist was falling in my eyes as the old white-bearded man smiled at me. We embraced with great affection and then kissed each other on the cheek. Turning around, he appeared to wipe a tear from his eye. Then he turned back toward me and removed his black top hat. With a broad grin and a flip of his wrist, he snapped its brim and instantly a pair of long asses' ears shot out from either side of it! Rolling his head from side to side with clownish humor, he placed the black top hat with its long asses' ears on my head. Then bowing deeply, he turned and with "a leap, a whistle and a fart" disappeared into the forest.

The End
of
HOLY
FOOLS
?

A FOOL'S LICENSE

Be it hereby known to one and all, Lords and Ladies, Pickpockets and Priests, Bellhops and Bishops, Night Watchmen and Guardians of Public Order, Mental Health Inspectors and Psychologists, that the bearer of this license,

_____

(print or write name in crayon)

has finished the required reading, practiced the specified exercises and passed the final examination to become a Holy Fool and Mad Hatter. Furthermore, the above said fool has graduated with full honors, *Magna Coon Loudly*. Having excelled in study, the bearer of this license now has the privilege to practice the art of Tom Foolery in all fifty of the United States. As a Cosmopolite, a citizen of the cosmos, the bearer of this license holds a global certificate to be foolish anywhere on Planet Earth (to practice silliness in space does require an additional permit from NASA).

This Fool's License is fully ecumenical, valid in all the churches of Christianity and in all places of worship and study of any of the world's religions. No extra church board permission, tribal permit, Zen stamp or papal indult is required to appear foolish in any church, mosque, synagogue, temple or shrine by taking God's words seriously and loving all peoples as yourself.

By the authority vested in me by the Divine Comedy, the Universal Holy Orders and all Local Unions of Fools, Clowns & Jesters, I solemnly attest to the validity of this Fool's License and to the professional standing of the person whose name appears above in freely practicing the Sacred Art of Foolishness.

Window Sill

Window Sill (*alias* Cellar Door)

Signed under the full of moon of April 1st and witnessed by a flock of passing loons.